TWAYNE'S WORLD AUTHORS SERIES

A Survey of the World's Literature

SPAIN

Janet W. Diaz, Texas Tech University

EDITOR

Gertrudis Gómez de Avellaneda

TWAS 599

Gertrudis Gómez de Avellaneda, 1851

GERTRUDIS GÓMEZ DE AVELLANEDA

By HUGH A. HARTER

Ohio Wesleyan University

TWAYNE PUBLISHERS

A DIVISION OF G. K. HALL & CO., BOSTON

Published in 1981 by Twayne Publishers,
A Division of G. K. Hall & Co.

Printed on permanent/durable acid-free paper and bound
in the United States of America

First Printing

Library of Congress Cataloging in Publication Data

Harter, Hugh A
Gertrudis Gómez de Avellaneda.

(Twayne's world authors series ; TWAS 599 : Spain)
Bibliography: p. 175
Includes index.
1. Gómez de Avellaneda y Arteaga, Gertrudis, 1814–1873
—Criticism and interpretation.
PG6525.H37   868′.5′09   80–22136
ISBN O–8057–6441–0

For Frannie, for happiness and love

Contents

About the Author

Hugh A. Harter is Professor of Romance Languages and holds the Chair of Robert Hayward Professor of French at Ohio Wesleyan University. He chaired the department from 1966 to 1980. He has degrees in both Spanish and French. He has traveled widely and has studied and taught in Spain, Latin America, France and North Africa. He founded and has been director of Programas Americanos in Segovia, Spain, since 1968. He served with Military Intelligence in France in World War II.

Among other grants, Professor Harter has been the recipient of a postdoctoral Andrew Mellon Fellowship at the University of Pittsburgh, and more recently of a US-Spanish Joint Committee for Educational and Cultural Affairs award to translate Nobel Prize winner Vicente Aleixandre's volume of poetry entitled *Sombra del paraíso*. He is currently completing translations of two novels by Moroccan author Driss Chraibi, and la Avellaneda's abolitionist novel *Sab*. He has taught at Wesleyan University in Connecticut, Chatham College in Pittsburgh, and Loyola University in Chicago. He has been visiting lecturer at universities in Peru and Spain. His publications, speeches, articles and reviews cover various aspects of Spanish, French, Latin American, and North African literature and culture.

Preface

In whatever other areas the women's movement of the 1970s may lay claim to accomplishments, the field of literature is in its debt for having jolted scholars into a recognition that some major women writers have been grievously neglected and are in dire need of being dusted off and placed in their proper niche in literary history. George Sand is a case in point. In less than five years time, three excellent books about her have appeared in English, and are being read by both public and specialist.

It is high time that the reputation of Gertrudis Gómez de Avellaneda received like treatment. It has been half a century since the only serious book-length study of this remarkable Cuban-born writer was published. In the intervening years, her dramas have been scrutinized in two doctoral dissertations and two women have written biographies of her. Otherwise she has been largely forgotten. She is almost wholly unknown to the English-speaking public, and this book, consequently, will be the first volume about her in English. Her reputation today, even among Hispanists, has survived only through a few anthologized poems. Her dramas are rarely mentioned, and her novels and shorter prose works, with the exception of the abolitionist novel *Sab* that was recently republished, lie unread and unstudied. Such neglect is not defensible in the face of la Avellaneda's fascinating life and her spectacularly successful career in nineteenth-century letters. No serious study of Spanish poetry, drama, or the novel can justifiably ignore her contributions and achievements in the middle decades of the last century without distorting the true picture. Her formidable career as a playwright may well be unsurpassed, if equalled, by any other woman in the history of the theater. In her own day, such well-known authors as Zorrilla, Juan Valera, Nicasio Gallego, Gil y Carrasco, and Pastor Díaz saw her as an extraordinary, even phenomenal, figure. She was publicly acclaimed the greatest woman poet of all Spanish literature. Her plays opened to full houses in which sat the royal family and the most prominent personnages of the time, and for the most part they had unusually long runs. The author herself received honor after honor. When she returned to her native Cuba in 1860 after twenty-four years' absence she was given a hero's welcome wherever she went. She may be said to epitomize romanticism, oscillating between the extremes of passionate love and religious devotion, the fevers of the flesh and the fervors of prayer, intense participation in life and temporary withdrawals into melancholy disenchantment, but always burning and consuming herself with the necessity to create, the obsession with the written word that lasted from early childhood to the final months of illness and premature death.

Her writings run to six large volumes in the 1914 Centennial edition, and subsequently other works have been published separately. The range of her writings is as impressive as the quality of most of her works. She excelled in the control and use of verse, whether lyrical or dramatic. She tried her hand successfully at all the genres and meters in vogue in and before her time. She was equally versatile in the field of drama. She wrote tragedies, straight dramas, comedies, and one farce. She has been judged less competent in the novel, but this assessment has become a kind of critical truism that is highly questionable. The fact is that her novels have yet to receive any serious consideration. Her treatment in them of such themes as slavery, woman in society and the family, marriage and divorce, criminal justice, the growing materialism of her times, and the like, make her novels meaningful to us in a way that the medievalist novels written by her contemporaries are not. In her shorter prose works, she clearly displays her skills as a story-teller. Her plots seem melodramatic to us today and her characters overdrawn, but they are particularly interesting as we perceive the reality of la Avellaneda's experiences behind them, and her use of dialogue is masterful.

Given the dearth of critical studies of la Avellaneda's work, the problem of bibliography has been vexing, although several of the secondary sources I have listed are helpful and insightful. Much more remains to be done to comprehend this woman whose struggle for women's rights, for justice, and whose interest in a whole range of social problems are very much part of our present concerns. This book should serve to bring her to the attention of students and teachers alike, and to women's study groups, whether of Hispanic background or not.

I am indebted to my wife Frances for her patience and gentle help, and for her reading and suggestions. Her growing excitement over la Avellaneda and her works has provided an additional and valuable stimulus in the preparation of the manuscript. I also wish to thank Dr. Donald Lenfest and Mrs. Claire Lenfest for their help in the final stages, and Professor Libuse Reed for her informed suggestions.

HUGH A. HARTER

Ohio Wesleyan University

Chronology

1814   March 23, birth of Gertrudis Gómez de Avellaneda in Puerto Príncipe in the central part of Cuba (Camagüey Province) to doña Francisca de Arteaga y Betancourt of Camagüey and the Spanish naval officer don Manuel Gómez de Avellaneda y Gil de Taboada. Gertrudis is nicknamed "Tula."

1823   Death of la Avellaneda's father early in the year. Ten months later doña Francisca marries a Spanish army officer, don Isidro de Escalada.

1826   Family arranges an engagement for Gertrudis to an older well-to-do cousin; she breaks engagement.

1833   Return of Escalada to Puerto Príncipe after lengthy intermittent absences. Family moves to Santiago de Cuba in preparation for a change of residence to Spain.

1836   Family departs for Europe. La Avellaneda writes the sonnet "Al partir." After a stay in Bordeaux, the family goes to reside with the Escaladas in La Coruña.

1837   Brief engagement to Ricafort. Family moves to Vigo.

1838   La Avellaneda and her brother Manuel travel via Lisbon and Cádiz to Constantina de la Sierra, and then to Seville where they set up residence. Publishes first poems under the pen name of "La Peregrina." Rejects her suitor Méndez Vigo, and meets Ignacio de Cepeda.

1839   First of the "love letters" to Cepeda.

1840   First play, *Leoncia*, is produced in Seville. Moves her residence to Madrid where she is introduced to the most prominent literary figures of the capital.

1841   First volume of poetry, *Poesías*. First novel, *Sab*, is published.

1842   *Dos mujeres* (novel).

1843   Ode written for Queen Isabel II's coming-of-age. Appearance of first "autobiography."

1844   Tragedy *Munio Alfonso* produced. *Espatolino* (novel)
       appears in serial form, and the short prose legend, *La
       Baroness de Joux*. Begins love affair with the poet Gabriel
       García Tassara.

1845   Tragedy *El Príncipe de Viana* produced. Wins both prizes
       of the prestigious Liceo of Madrid. Birth of an illegitimate
       daughter named Brenhilde who dies in infancy.

1846   Serial publication of *Guatimozín, último emperador de
       México*. Marries don Pedro Sabater, who dies in France
       less than four months later. Tragedy *Egilona* produced.

1847   Seeks solace in a convent in Bordeaux and writes a *Devo-
       cionario*.

1849   "La velada del helecho o el donativo del diablo" (No-
       vella). Summer at the Escorial. Triumphal opening of
       the biblical tragedy *Saúl*.

1850   Second and larger volume of *Poesías*. Writes the legend
       "La ondina del lago azul" and the novel *Dolores*.

1851   *Dolores* and the legend "La montaña maldita" published.

1852   Production of five plays: *La verdad vence apariencias,
       Errores del corazón, El donativo del diablo, La hija de las
       flores*, and the short *loa* on which she collaborated.

1853   Applies for membership in the Royal Spanish Academy
       and is refused entry because she is a woman. Two dramas,
       La aventurera and *Hortensia*, produced.

1854   Death of la Avellaneda's half-sister. Cepeda marries.

1855   Opening of two one-act plays, *Simpatía y antipatía* and
       La hija del rey René, and of the full-length drama *Oráculos
       de Talía o los duendes en el palacio*. Participates in the
       public "crowning" of the poet Quintana. Marries Colonel
       Domingo Verdugo y Massieu in the royal palace of
       Madrid.

1858   Opening of the drama *Tres amores* and of the biblical
       tragedy *Baltasar*. Colonel Verdugo stabbed and seriously
       wounded. Convalescent journey of the Verdugos through
       the Pyrenees region to Barcelona and Valencia. Tula
       gathers material for her Basque legends.

1859   Second trip to northern Spain and the Pyrenees area of
       France. Writes "La ondina del lago azul." Colonel Verdugo
       named to the staff of the new governor-general of Cuba.
       Departure for Cuba. Writes "La vuelta a la patria."

Chronology

1860 "Crowning" of la Avellaneda in the Teatro Tacón in Havana. Founds and edits the short-lived *Album cubano* and publishes several short prose works in it. Visits Puerto Príncipe.

1861 *El artista barquero o los cuatro cinco de julio,* and the shorter prose works "El aura blanco" and "El cacique de Turmequé."

1863 Colonel Verdugo dies at age forty-six.

1864 Tula leaves Cuba. Visits New York and Niagara Falls. Travels to London and Paris before returning to Spain. Remains in Seville for four years.

1867 Returns to Madrid and visits Manuel in Paris.

1868 Revolution and overthrow of Isabel II. Brother Manuel dies.

1869 Moves to Madrid. Begins publication of her *Obras,* which she herself edited and chose, through 1871. Writes two plays, neither produced: *Catalina* and *El millonario y la maleta.*

1873 La Avellaneda dies of diabetes on February 1.

1914 Centennial celebrations in Havana and publication of an expanded edition of Tula's *Obras.*

CHAPTER 1

Life and Career

ON the centennial of her birth in 1914, Gertrudis Gómez de
Avellaneda y Arteaga was acclaimed as a rival of some of
the greatest writers of Spanish literature, of Fray Luis de León,
Herrera, and Quintana in the field of poetry, and of Lope de
Vega and Calderón de la Barca in drama.[1] We would hardly
make such extravagant claims today, but the obscurity to which,
ironically enough, she has been relegated a little over a century
after her death is even less equitable given her very real talents
and accomplishments. In the decades of the 1840s and 1850s
when she was at the height of her powers, la Avellaneda—she is
frequently referred to by this name or by the nickname Tula
which she often used to sign correspondence with friends and
family—went from one triumph to another, from ovation and
laurel-crowning to repeated accolades from public and critics
alike. The publication of her poems, novels and travel articles
constituted an event; the openings of her plays were major
occasions, attended by the royal family as well as notables of
the political, social, and literary world. Her dark beauty as a
young woman, and later on as a stately matron, is still striking
to us today as we see her in portraits and engravings. It is not
surprising that when the lovely Tula first appeared in the literary
circles of Madrid in 1840, twenty-five years old and the bearer
of a letter of recommendation from the venerable don Alberto
Lista, she dazzled the most distinguished writers of the capital.
She also soon caused malicious tongues to wag, and not wholly
without reason.

We know that la Avellaneda was an admirer of George Sand,
Tula's senior by a scant ten years, and in many ways she herself
might be dubbed the George Sand of Hispanic literature, both

17

in her assertive feminism and in her position as a major figure
of nineteenth-century letters. Her literary output was smaller,
and her amorous adventures less overt and spectacular than those
of her famous contemporary, but if Sand was the outstanding
woman writer of the century in France, la Avellaneda could
justifiably lay claim to the title in the Hispanic world, despite
such formidable contenders as Carolina Coronado and Rosalía
de Castro in poetry, and Fernán Caballero and the Countess
Pardo Bazán in the novel. For all the excellence of their accomplishments, none of these women can match Tula in breadth and
variety of literary achievement. In form and in substance, her
range was very impressive, in poetry, the drama, the novel, the
short story and legend, the essay, and the epistle. None of the
famous men who admired her questioned her ability. When she
applied for admittance to the prestigious Royal Academy on the
death of her friend Juan Nicasio Gallego, she was denied entry
on the grounds that she was a woman. A subsequent polling
of the members of the Academy showed conclusively that la
Avellaneda was considered by them to be eminently deserving
of election to the vacant seat by virtue of her literary achievements. Her exclusion was decided solely on the basis of her sex.

Various factors, which we shall discuss in their place, undoubtedly contributed to la Avellaneda's relegation to an ill-
merited obscurity. One of them was an unfortunate debate by
scholars and literati over the question of the author's patriotic
affinities. Was she loyal to the Cuba of her birth or to the Spain
where she had enjoyed her major triumphs? It was one of those
literary quarrels which reflect contemporary politics and conflicts
but which are unrelated to the realm of aesthetics. No such
dichotomy existed in fact, for Tula remained profoundly at-
tached to the soil which gave her birth; but she was also very
much a part of the artistic and intellectual world of Madrid
for a major part of her adult life. Furthermore, Cuba was still
a colony and considered an integral part of Spain in her life-
time. The accusation that she had turned her back on Cuba
was one that hurt her deeply, and she strongly denied it. Tula's
family, like her character, exemplifies the union of the Hispanic
world. Her mother was of a well-to-do patrician family long
established in Cuba, and her father was of an aristocratic but

impoverished line mentioned in the chronicles of Spain from the time of the reconquest from the Moors, or so the daughter was to claim.

I *Childhood*

La Avellaneda was born in Puerto Príncipe in the central part of Cuba on March 23, 1814. She was baptised on April 1 as María Gertrudis de los Dolores, although the poetess herself, perhaps from coquetry, was later to make herself two years younger in her autobiographical writings. Her mother, doña Francisca de Arteaga y Betancourt, of Spanish descent, belonged to a family that long had distinguished itself in Puerto Príncipe. We may suppose that something of that family was transformed into a fictional portrait in la Avellaneda's first novel *Sab*. The father, don Manuel Gómez de Avellaneda, was of a noble Spanish family that could claim descent from the royal family of Navarre and the high artistocracy of Vizcaya, a heritage of which his daughter was cognizant and duly proud. He had come to Cuba in 1809 as naval lieutenant and was named commander of the Spanish fleet in the central part of the island. Although it had been customary for the commanding officer to live in the port of Nuevitas, don Manuel decided to reside in nearby Puerto Príncipe, a larger and more habitable center in the area of Camagüey.

The city of Puerto Príncipe in which doña Gertrudis grew up lies in the center of Cuba, about halfway from either coast. It is on a high plain or savannah surrounded by two small rivers, in a region rich in agriculture (sugar, coffee, corn, rice, and tobacco) and in cattle. It had been colonized since the sixteenth century, prospering despite raids and sackings at intervals by English and Dutch pirates. Also noted for the abundance of its flowers, the excellence of its honey and of its fruit, it cultivated especially the guava apple, from which an industry in preserves developed. In the year 1800, the high court or *Audiencia* of the Caribbean had been transferred from Santo Domingo to Puerto Príncipe, where it remained until 1838, functioning also as the seat of the only appellate court on the island. At the time of the arrival of Tula's future father in 1809, the population was about

30,000 inhabitants, quite a large city for its day, of which some 12,000 were blacks, either freedmen or slaves.

Don Manuel had been in Puerto Príncipe three years when he met, courted, and married the poetess's mother. The marriage was to last only a decade, producing five children, only two of whom, Gertrudis, the eldest, and a brother Manuel, three years her junior, survived infancy and were alive at the time of the father's death in 1823. Much later, in one of her autobiographical writings, Gertrudis was to describe her parents' marriage as unhappy for doña Francisca because of the marked difference in age of the spouses, but she defends her mother as "the most faithful and virtuous of wives."[2] Whatever the truth of this, the young, beautiful, and wealthy widow waited a shockingly short time before giving her hand in marriage a second time. Less than ten months after the death of her first husband, and much against the wishes of her family, she took a new husband, don Isidoro de Escalada. A lieutenant colonel stationed in Puerto Príncipe, he came from an old family originally from the area of Burgos in northern Spain. The wedding took place in November of 1823 when Tula was nine years old. Her first verses, she later declared, were written at this time in memory of her dead father. His memory was to have deep meaning for her, and his reiterated desire that his children know his native Andalusia was one that the daughter was to conserve tenaciously until the trip was finally made.

Meanwhile the child prodigy was developing. She was being educated by tutors, not unusual for a provincial city of Cuba in that period when there was a marked scarcity of teachers. Geography and history were of no interest to her, but she rapidly learned French and at a very early age was already a voracious reader. Puerto Príncipe in the 1820s, despite its prosperity, was hardly a cultural center. Nevertheless, books were available, and the already irrepressible Tula indulged her growing passion for poetry, drama, and the novel. She admits that her every whim was humored and that she was badly spoiled. She was, after all, the eldest, and the stepfather who might have disciplined her was conveniently absent much of the time on military duty. The mother's attempts to steer her daughter toward more acceptably feminine interests such as drawing and music came to little.

Tula was different. She had no interest in the games of children her age, and gave her friendship only to a couple of girl cousins, and with them she shared the reading of novels, poetry, and plays. Reading became, according to her autobiographical writings, "our dominant passion." We may well suppose that it was the "spoiled" and often melancholy and pensive Tula who led the way and insisted on intellectual rather than more mundane pursuits for three budding young girls. When she was thirteen her mother was still trying in vain to modify her obsession with reading and her avoidance of "society."

Obviously there was enough to vex a mother in a small provincial city where the do's and don'ts of children were narrowly circumscribed. At age twelve, la Avellaneda was daily writing odes in imitation of the poet Quintana, and just as rapidly burning them as unsatisfactory. She also directed plays, assigning lesser roles to her little friends and keeping the major male roles for herself. At this time also, this child prodigy wrote a novel and a tragedy entitled *Hernando Cortez,* a subject to which she was to return later in a novel on the conquest of Mexico. She burned both works, as she later declared in Madrid to her author-friend Nicomedes Pastor Díaz. By age fifteen, the passion for reading plays—there were no productions for her to see—became her obsession. She read not only Spanish drama, but French as well. If we are to believe her later declarations about her youth, she was already reciting whole passages of Corneille and Racine from memory by the time she was an adolescent. During this period also, Tula had the good fortune to have among her tutors one of Cuba's most famous poets, the "singer of Niagara," José María Heredia, who had come to Puerto Príncipe to begin his career as a lawyer. His influence on his young charge's future poetic creation was a lasting one.

II *The Young Woman*

The age had come, however, for Tula to become a young woman. She tells us that she abandoned books and studies only to devote herself with equal intensity and application to clothes, dances, and parties. Instead of ordering new publications from Europe, she now asked for the latest fashions. Her mother and stepfather decided that the time had come for marriage, and Tula was engaged to a well-to-do distant relative. It was a good match, but just before the marriage, the bride-to-be changed her mind and refused to marry the man. The ensuing bad feelings caused deep ruptures within the family and lost Tula's grandfather's inheritance for her mother. The family quarrels and recriminations took a deep toll on the young woman who became ill, writing later that so deep was her depression that only her religious principles and love for her mother and her brother Manuel kept her from attempting suicide. Arranged marriages, emotional illness, and suicide repeatedly appear in her works.

By the age of eighteen she could play waltzes on the piano, sing some arias of Rossini, and do inept paintings of flowers. She had learned almost nothing of mathematics or of grammar. Nevertheless, she tells us, "I wrote and spoke with more exactitude than is common in my country and despite my innate disdain for learning, I had an avid thirst for knowing, and I thought a great deal."[3] Tula returned to her reading, of history, magazines, and novels, saturating herself with the French authors in vogue. She devoured the vivid and emotionally dramatic tales of Chateaubriand with their descriptions of the vast panoramas of the New World in *Atala,* the neurasthenic and quasi-incestuous loves of *René,* and Victor Hugo's medieval *Our Lady of Paris.* She discovered the early works—*Indiana* and *Valentina*—of the woman whom some asserted Tula herself took as a model, Aurore Dupin, known to the world as George Sand. She was also then reading the novels of Sir Walter Scott, the poems and dramas of Lord Byron, which she had in French translation, and the poetry of the melancholy Lamartine of "The Lake" and the "Meditations."[4] As her literary horizons broadened, so did her desire to see the Europe from which her reading matter came, a desire, she wrote in 1839, that had been with her since early childhood and which her father had strongly reinforced in her with his tales of his native Andalusia and Seville.

Before don Manuel's death, this idea of returning to Spain and taking his children with him had become almost obsessive, as had his fears that the rebellion and takeover by blacks in Haiti would soon be the fate of Cuba. It was not until 1836, thirteen

years after the death of the father, that his wish was to be fulfilled. It was also after some heated arguments between Tula
and her stepfather on the one side, and the mother, reluctant to
leave her native Camagüey, on the other. Finally, the family
went to Havana for several months before embarking for France,
and there the woman triumphed in the ballroom as did the
poetess with her verses. She was courted, flattered, and admired.

III *The Voyage to Europe*

In April, 1836, the family embarked on a French frigate, the
Belochan, bound for Bordeaux. La Avellaneda was never to
forget that first crossing of which she has left lyrical descriptions
in her autobiographical writings and one of her best known
poems, the sonnet to Cuba, "Al partir" ("On Leaving") that
begins with the line "Perla del mar" ("Pearl of the sea"). She
writes of her mixed feelings as she left her friends and family,
and the exaltation she felt as the ship moved out across the vast
and moonlit sea. With even more passion she describes what
she felt when, off the coast of Bermuda, the ship was caught in
a hurricane. As the ship was tossed "up to the clouds and then
submerged in the abysses," the tempestuous Gertrudis, unlike
her fellow passengers who were seized with terror, was thrilled
with the danger and the terrible spectacle. She tells us that her
actions were the subject of conversation for days afterward,
relating, that by the light of the lightning flashes that filled the
black sky she recited a section of Heredia's poem "A Niagara"
("To Niagara") that begins: "Al despenarse el huracán furioso, /
al retumbar sobre mi frente el rayo / palpitando gocé. . . ." ("As
the fury of the hurricane broke forth, / and on my brow the
lightning fell / I felt my heart leap up. . . .") It was as though
the tempests of her reading had become reality.

After almost two months at sea, the ship reached its destina-
tion. The family spent eighteen days in Bordeaux. Tula went
sightseeing, attended the theater and opera, and visited the
château and woods where Montesquieu had lived, worked, and
written his *Spirit of Laws* which she had already read in Cuba.
She also began the writing of her first published novel, *Sab,*
before the family embarked for La Coruña on the North Atlantic

coast of Galicia and the home of don Isidoro Escalada, her step-father.

Tula reacted badly both to the climate of the northwest coast, cold and rainy in contrast to the tropical skies and sunshine of Cuba, and to the dour character of the people. She disliked the way they pronounced Castilian; she deplored the poverty and the beggars in the streets, the lack of fine buildings, or of even a fine church or a good theater. She did, however, learn to enjoy the *paseo* on foot which differed from Cuba's *paseo* in carriages. Her initial dislike of the city, plus her temperament and her intellect, soon brought her, along with her mother and brother, into conflict with her stepfather's family who scornfully called her the "Doctor" and the "atheist." She took refuge in writing the novel *Sab*, and she was courted by the son of the former governor-general of Cuba, don Mariano Ricafort. She must have known her suitor, Francisco, several years earlier in Cuba. At any rate, whether from real attraction, from boredom, or as an escape from the household where she was restricted and ridi-culed, she became engaged to Ricafort. The marriage did not take place. Escalada refused to give her inheritance to his step-daughter as she was still not of age. She refused to go to her new family "as a beggar," and the project came to nothing. Rica-fort went off to the Carlist wars then raging in the Basque country, and the talented Tula recognized that her fiancé had not been right for her: he disliked her studying and her writing of poetry.

Meanwhile, Manuel had come home, and the mother decided that it would be best to separate the children from her husband's family. Consequently, a journey, which la Avellaneda was later to describe in her *Memoirs*, was undertaken by litter and by carriage, through Pontevedra to Vigo. In Vigo the brother and sister finally succeeded in persuading their mother to give her permission for them to travel to the south, to the little town of Constantina to see the family of their long-dead father.

IV *The Move to Andalusia*

On April 5, 1838, the two embarked on an English steamer, the *Londonderry*. Tula had mixed feelings once again—the excitement of the trip along with the sadness at leaving her mother for the first time—but she was glad to be away from Galicia. Two days later she visited Lisbon, and then went on to Cadiz for a stay of almost a week. Cadiz with its cathedral, squares, and flowers pleased her. From there another boat took brother and sister to Seville, where they took a carriage overland to Constantina de la Sierra, some forty-four miles away. Unfortunately, the town was a disappointment. It had a population of some 4,000 inhabitants whose lives were tied to the agriculture and products of the region: olive oil, wine, and brandy. The streets were dirty and unpaved, with little of commerce or industry. Only the countryside around it lent a saving grace. It was spring when Manuel and Gertrudis arrived, and the fields and woods were beautiful. The two "orphans" went to live with their aged and childless uncle, don Felipe Gómez de Avellaneda, who received them with much affection. He undertook to arrange a marriage for his niece with a wealthy young man from Constantina who had asked for her hand. Once more Tula flatly refused to be married, and so, after a short three months in the paternal home, she and Manuel left to take up residence in Seville.

V *Residence in Seville*

Tula wrote later that "I had a world inside my head that was not the real world! Life and people were not the way I had imagined them. I began to suffer. A painful and prosaic period was beginning for me, one whose unpleasant details I cannot relate today." Fortunately for the two young persons, who were almost destitute, doña Francisca, seeing that her husband had been called to duty in the zone of the fighting in the north, came to Seville also and took a large and comfortable house. It was a rather large family; in addition to doña Francisca and her two eldest children, Gertrudis, now twenty-four, and Manuel, twenty-two, there were her three by Escalada, Felipe, aged twelve, Pepita, aged ten, and Emilio who was eight. La Avellaneda has left a fairly detailed description of the Seville of those days, the city in which, one might say, her life was to begin to take definitive shape. "I can hardly tell you," she wrote, "the magic of this Seville in whose arabesque streets, narrow and twisting as they are, one seems to always find something new even though we go through them daily."[5] She writes at length of the beauties of the city, of the houses, the patios, the potted flowers, the great squares, the famous streets, the theater, the Alcazar, and the cathedral. There was an elegant and active social life, as well as long-established literary and cultural activity in Seville. Excellent bookstores imported English and French books, and sold books, magazines, and papers from all over Spain. The journalistic publications in Seville itself included one in which the young poetess published a poem, "El Cisne" ("The Swan"). This review's editor was Juan José Bueno, and its collaborators included José Amador de los Ríos and Gabriel García Tassara.

Soon the beauty and the talents of the exotic Cuban were known to all the city. Tula's home became a meeting place for the aristocratic and the talented young people of Seville. Among the portraits of Tula from this period, one shows a dark-haired, dark-eyed woman whose tendency to corpulence had not yet marred her attractiveness. She declaimed well, reading her own poetry—both that written in Cuba and what she was writing at the time—in a mellifluent voice. In addition to the admiration these recitings caused, she also roused amorous excitement. The results were more serious than a flirtatious young woman might have wished. One affair almost ended badly when a young man of a wealthy and distinguished family of Seville, Antonio Méndez Vigo, fell madly in love with Gertrudis. She was not insensitive to the passion he declared for her, as she was to reminisce later in her letters.[6] "Poor child," she called him, "how much he loved me! How did it happen that this capricious heart of mine was incapable of returning his feeling? I don't know." All she felt was what "a mother feels for her son." He was not her son, however, as she wrote later to the only man she herself ever fully loved. When young Antonio asked for Tula's hand and was refused, he threatened suicide, but finally left Seville to get over his dangerous passion.

VI *Ignacio de Cepeda*

At this time, however, Gertrudis was to meet her own Nemesis, two years younger than she, don Ignacio de Cepeda, a member of a rich and important family from the province of Seville, who was studying law at the time he met Tula. He has been described as modest, well-spoken, courteous, and pleasant, but also lacking in imagination, egotistical, cold, methodical, and materialistic in matters of money and possessions.[7] Another biographer of la Avellaneda, who described Cepeda as "a terribly normal man,"[8] goes on to say, perspicaciously, that "in that fact may have lain the enormous power of attraction that from the first moment on he held over the poetess, who admired in his spirit the tranquillity and balance that was lacking in her own." However accurate this observation, there is also the strong possibility that much of the continuing fascination of Cepeda for la Avellaneda also became, whether consciously or not, a question of wills. The forty letters, which, over a period from 1839 to 1854, she wrote to her reluctant lover, now constitute a literary treasure as well as a penetrating autobiographical and psychological document that we shall treat later on as a part of la Avellaneda's writings. For any study of the poetess's life they are a major source of information, revealing what must be considered as her most profound emotional involvement and providing a key for understanding both her life and her literary works.

Various reasons have been advanced for Cepeda's refusal to marry Tula, the main one being that she was not rich enough for him. She was, however, from a distinguished family, and she did have an inheritance from her father—and later, from her father's family. She was young and beautiful, already on the way to the fame to which Cepeda was not insensitive. By the time the correspondence ended, some fourteen years after it began, Tula had become a very famous woman, and it was surely this fact that led Cepeda to put in his will a clause directing his wife to have the letters published at his expense after his death.

A more probable reason for Cepeda's not marrying the impetuous and passionate Gertrudis was her unconventionality and her aggressiveness. He seems to have been at times attracted and even entranced by la Avellaneda, but the letters indicate an equal propensity to avoid a woman whose strength of character was a matter of considerable comment at various periods of her life. She was imperious, even when young. It is understandable that for a "very normal man," the potential torrent of emotion in this extraordinarily verbal woman must have been overwhelming and even frightening.

Tula herself had reason to be fearful of her emotions. In a letter of June, 1839, a year after the "friendship" had begun, she wrote: "I hope once to find on this earth a heart that is as melancholy, ardent, proud, and ambitious as is my own; to share with him my pleasures and pains and give him excess of life that I can not stand all alone. But more frequently I fear within myself this immense faculty for suffering, and I have a presentiment that a vehement love would stir up tempests in my breast that would even disorder my reason and life."[9] How prophetic this was the authoress was soon to learn. Her love for Cepeda, and his pattern of acceptance-rejection, was to change la Avellaneda's life completely, as is reflected in passages and situations in her novels and plays as well as in the epistolatory body of her writings. The struggle to control the volcanic emotions she felt is apparent in the letters; in many of them the superficial reason or pretext for writing barely masks the feeling, and in others, she openly begs her lover for forgiveness for outbursts of temperament.[10]

The "friendship" was not sufficiently tempestuous to keep Tula from writing, however. Seeking solace in her work, she went to Cadiz to meet the publishers of a literary magazine called *La Aureola* in which she had published some poems under the pseudonym of "La Peregrina" ("The Wanderer"). During this period also she met in Seville the renowned Alberto Lista, poet and teacher, and friend of poets. She was reading voraciously, as always. A list that she sent to Cepeda as a co-reading project gives a succinct picture of her preferences at the time; she was writing her first novel *Sab* and much of the poetry that was to constitute her first volume of verse. The list includes Sir Walter Scott's *The Pirates, Kenilworth, Waverly* and *The Antiquary*, Madame de Staël's *Corinne*, Chateaubriand's *Atala*, and the poetry of Alberto Lista, Manuel José Quintana, and José María de Heredia.[11] To carry out this joint reading, the reticent Cepeda finally agreed to see his *innamorata* once a week. It is at this point that the stiff and formal—and rigidly repeated—"usted" of the letters gives way to the "tú" form of address. However, Tula quotes a line from a play of Moreto to make a point: "What a luke-warm suitor you are!"[12] The results of the love affair for Tula were suffering, torment, jealousies, and a heart that more and more dominated her head and doings. Finally she could neither write nor read; she could not even do such prosaic things as embroider. By January of 1840, she spoke of never seeing Cepeda again.

Despite her anguish, and to a degree utilizing it, she did begin writing. She succeeded in writing two acts of her play *Leoncia*, but she was also acting out her own drama of temper and jealousy for which she would humbly beg pardon in one of the letters. We may conjecture that she had created a scene at a theatrical performance, one that the conservative and tepid lover saw as an opportunity to withdraw even more. By March or April of 1840, the complete break was near or had already taken place. Tula's letter and pleadings were in vain. She writes of death, of leaving "this horrible life, this world,"[13] and in a poem entitled "Amor y orgullo" ("Love and Pride") paints a self-portrait of the "Que en triste abandono / Su amante la deja, / De bronce a su queja, / De hielo a su ardor" ("sad abandonment in which / her love leaves her, / bronze to her lament, / ice to her ardor.")[14]

Despite the brutal ruptures in this love affair, we might say that for la Avellaneda it was never truly over. The cautious protestation of Platonic and fraternal friendship and the declarations that passion had been calmed into forms of a more lasting and tranquil relationship seem specious. Perhaps she meant what she was writing, but soon the truce is broken and the letters begin again to wrangle and argue. They also give us clear information about what Gertrudis was working on.

In August, 1839, Tula had finished a translation from the French of a poem by Lamartine entitled "The Fountain," was translating Millevoye's "The Anniversary," and had sent off the former to *La Aureola*. In the same letter, she states that she had read the first ten chapters of *Sab* to friends. and had already found twenty "subscribers" to help with the printing costs for publication of the novel. Subscriptions had also come in from Granada and from Malaga, so we know that la Avellaneda was by this time a regional celebrity. From as far as Valencia, requests were received for her writings. *Leoncia* was finished and in production in Seville, and Tula proudly informed Cepeda that the play was asked for by producers in Granada, Malaga and Valencia.

The opening of *Leoncia* was twice postponed, as Tula wanted Cepeda to come from his mountain retreat to the opening. He did not comply, and finally the premiere was held on June 6, 1840. The play received excellent reviews, and soon there were successful productions in both Cadiz and Granada. A news report of the play in Madrid mentions the authoress only as "The Wanderer" and gives both the drama and the production high praise.[15] The basic theme of passion and jealousy reflects the mood of the authoress at the time of inception.

VII   *The Move to Madrid*

In the meantime, both an aunt and an uncle on Tula's father's side died, willing everything to Gertrudis and her brother Manuel. The love affair with Cepeda presumably over, Tula decided to move to Madrid ,which she did sometime in the summer of 1840, taking with her Manuel and a woman relative. Her mother remained in Seville with the younger children, and her poet-daughter sent her a poem for New Year's 1841.

Alberto Lista had given Gertrudis a letter of introduction to don Juan Nicasio Gallego, and soon literary Madrid was at her feet. Her combination of physical beauty with unusual talent astounded the establishment "greats" of the period. Gallego reminisced: "How great was our astonishment when we met a young woman of twenty-five, extremely gracious, full of life and very attractive!"[16] Another description, by Nicomedes Pastor Díaz, is even more succinct: "The most distinguished writers of the capital, without distinction of age or school, surrounded her from then on with tributes of friendship and enthusiasm which they rendered exclusively to talent, inspiration, and genius. The duke of Frías, don Juan Nicasio Gallego, don Manuel Quintana, Espronceda, Zorrilla, García Tassara, Roca de Togores, Pastor Díaz, Bretón, Hartzenbusch, and many other writers of major or minor reputation have been ever since her devoted friends or fervent admirers."[17]

The primary literary club of Madrid, the recently founded

Liceo de Madrid, welcomed her. José Zorrilla presented her, terming her Spain's first poetess. In his memoirs written years later, he recalled the night that he first read a poem of hers to the *Liceo* and remembered her dark and statuesque beauty. Descriptions have come down to us of her own readings to literary groups, which must have been impressive. Such contacts were stimulating for la Avellaneda, who was then writing more poetry and preparing a volume of her verses. Among other works, she composed an elegy for her fellow Cuban José María Heredia, a poem as important for what it shows of Tula's love for Cuba as it does for the memory of one of the island's greatest and most patriotic poets. This work inaugurates a persistent and fairly important vein of "occasional" verses dedicated to poets she admired and knew.

She was a successful poet and playwright in 1841 when her first novel appeared. The "Indianist" and highly romantic *Sab* is a tale of unrequited passions set in Tula's native Cuba, and dedicated to Alberto Lista. Its theme of abolitionism was not popular in conservative circles and must have added to the controversies that increasingly plagued the young writer, and were to mar her later years. Her first book of poetry, *Poesías,* appeared at almost the same time, in 1841. The volume was dedicated to the poetess's mother, doña Francisca Arteaga de Escalada, and had a prologue written by Juan Nicasio Gallego. It contains forty-five poems in all, seven of them translations, dated from 1836 to 1841. Within a short time there appeared a second novel entitled *Dos mujeres,* (*Two Women*), published in 1842. Like the *Poesías* volume, it was dedicated to Gallego. Its principal theme, as with *Sab* and *Leoncia,* is passion and jealousy. Her own passions had not abated, but they were finding an outlet in literature.

The poems written for special occasions were growing in number. She wrote one after the death of José de Espronceda, another for a woman friend from Cadiz, and one that was to resound to her public fame, an ode composed for the celebration of the coming-of-age of Isabel II in 1843. The queen gave the poetess her hand to kiss, and thus Tula's friendship with the royal family was established. In 1844 she published a poem welcoming back the queen mother who had been forced into exile by the liberal party. Tula contributed an article on women to a Madrid magazine during this period and also wrote a biographical introduction to a book, *Viaje a la Habana* (*Trip to Havana*), first drafted in French and then translated into Spanish, by the Cuban-born countess of Merlin who resided in Paris.

It was at this time that the first biography of la Avellaneda appeared. Published in a magazine called *El Arlequín*, it was from the pen of Antonio Neira de Mosquera who had been in correspondence with the poetess. In a letter of February, 1843, Tula promises to send Neira copies of her novel *Sab*. Noting that the lithographs that have been done of her are not true likenesses, she declines to send one. She affirms that *Leoncia* was written in a period of eight days. It was in this letter that statements about her personal life appeared that have often been quoted since: "I am alone in the world, I live alone and am eccentric in many ways. Although I offend no one, I have enemies, and although I am not at all ambitious, I am accused of excessive pretensions. My family belongs to the class that is called nobility, but I belong to no class. I treat the duke the same as the actor. I recognize no other aristocracy than that of talent."[18]

In 1843 the irrepressible Gertrudis was planning a second drama. The play did not open until June of the following year, but the conception was one to which its author had given much thought and planning. Romantic drama by this time had come to dominate the theater, with neoclassical drama almost entirely forgotten. La Avellaneda, however, set out to fuse the two dramatic traditions, the dominant romanticism with the classical sense of tragedy. The result was a tragedy in four acts entitled *Munio Alfonso*, based—or so its author asserted—on historical fact, a tale of love and tragic consequences among her own ancestors. She dedicated her drama to her brother Manuel as the last living member of an illustrious line, of which the play's hero was one of its most famous representatives. The work was an immediate success. The author was called to the stage, applauded, and honored. The ovations continued night after night.

Some six months later, in January, 1844, the novel *Espatolino* began to appear in serial form in a Madrid magazine. This time the hero was a bandit chief, likewise a historical character. Historical fact, however, was softened and sentimentalized in the version that la Avellaneda gave to the Spanish reading public.

Some thought the novel was a translation. This was not the case, but the fictional work that followed it might be considered so. It was styled a "legend founded on the French" and was entitled *La baronesa de Joux (The Baroness of Joux)*. The year of publication, 1844, was also to see the premiere of one of la Avellaneda's major plays. The subject matter of the drama, as in the case of *Alfonso Munio*, was drawn from medieval Spanish history. The plot is based on the life of Prince Carlos of Navarre who lived in the fifteenth century and who was half-brother of the far more famous Ferdinand of Aragon. Similarly a tale of violent passions, it is placed within the framework of high political intrigue. The result was another success, although there were critics who found fault with it. Tula was again applauded on opening night and at her feet fell the now accustomed laurel crowns. The title that la Avellaneda gave to this play was *El Principe de Viana (The Prince of Viana)*. It too was categorized as a tragedy.

The year 1845 was to see one of la Avellaneda's greatest public triumphs. The youthful Queen Isabel II had, in a moment of spontaneous charity, pardoned several officers sentenced to death because of their participation in a conspiracy against the government. That act of the monarch was widely hailed, and it was decided that there should be a poetry contest to commemorate the matter. The *Liceo* of Madrid agreed to officiate and two prizes, a first and second of 6,000 and 3,000 *reales* respectively, were established. Only two poems of the number submitted were considered by the judges to be worthy of prizes. The first had been entered by one Felipe de Escalada and the second was signed by Gertrudis Gómez de Avellaneda. Both actually were the work of the same author who had used the name of her half-brother to enter the first poem. After a special meeting, it was decided that as the two were the only poems worthy of the prizes, both would go to la Avellaneda. A solemn ceremony was held in which the uncle of the queen, don Francisco de Paula, placed a crown of laurel and gold on Tula's head.

Several months later, in February of 1846, another novel began to appear in serial form. This one was based on a subject that had interested Tula since her adolescent years in Cuba: the conquest of Mexico. Its title was *Guatimocín, último emperador de México (Cuauhtemoc, The Last Aztec Emperor)*. Tula, we should recall, had written a play entitled *Hernán Cortés* (*Hernando Cortez*) at the age of twelve. The novel can be considered a culmination of that interest and of considerable reading about the conquest.

VIII *Tassara and Brenhilde*

Gertrudis at the age of thirty had scaled heights in the literary world to which few could aspire. She had published a volume of poetry and five novels, had three plays successfully produced, and had seen various articles and poems in print. She had triumphed in literature and seemingly had overcome her disappointment in love. The singularly most tragic drama of her life was, however, about to commence. It matches in intensity any of the dramatic scenes she had written or was to write, and the letters which have come down to us are heartrending in their pain and tragedy.

One of the young poets whom Gertrudis had met in Seville and who had moved to Madrid was Gabriel García Tassara. Two years Tula's junior, he was talented, handsome, and seemingly very much in love with the Cuban poetess. García Tassara courted her in verse, and by the spring of 1844, the affair had become more than just a literary relationship. A year later, la Avellaneda gave birth to a sickly daughter whom she called Brenhilde. The child was to live a short nine months. As the tormented mother's letters show, the father neither acknowledged paternity nor even came to see his offspring. The desperate letters that the mother sent to Tassara imploring him to come to her side give poignant testimony to the suffering Tula endured at this time.

Nevertheless, by the summer of 1845, she resumed her correspondence with Cepeda. She writes that although he thinks her happy and preoccupied only with her "glory," she is actually very much overworked and upset by the criticism, especially of women, and "villified by the slavery of society." She has become pessimistic and bitter: "Already old at the age of thirty, I foresee that it will be my lot to outlive myself, unless out of sheer weariness I suddenly leave this world that is so small, so insufficient in measuring out happiness, and so big and so overflowing when it comes to its bitterness."[19] It is also obvious that Cepeda knew something of what had happened between Tula and Tassara, for she defends her own actions, and says that she acted honorably. Interestingly enough, Tula was later to become friendly with Tassara again, to send him some books and letters, and to include a poem of his in her *Album Cubano*. It speaks well for her character that she could forgive and forget, even in the face of such treatment.

As Cepeda was thinking of marrying, Tula wrote to him about it, pretending to be the disinterested friend. In the same correspondence she declared that she herself would never marry, but that if she did, she would do so "with the blessing of a priest or without it."[20] Depressed, even confused as to her future, she writes of moving to Paris where she will earn more money, and affirms that she is tired of flattery and adulation, weary of malicious tongues and of life itself. She composed the poem "Al Escorial" ("To the Escorial"), a sonnet for the duke of Frías, and a birthday poem for the queen; she also traveled in the area of La Granja and Segovia. One poem, written at this time, "El genio de la melancolía" ("The Nature of Melancholy") was to live on in the verse of another, and more enduring nineteenth-century poet, in Gustavo Adolfo Bécquer's *Rima V*. Tula's poem, now less known than the latter, begins: "Yo soy quien murmura del río en las aguas, / rizando sus ondas de cándida espuma" ("I am he who in the river's waters murmurs, / ruffling its waves of snowy foam").[21]

IX *Marriage to Sabater*

Despite her statements about marriage, however, la Avellaneda soon became a bride. The circumstances of her decision make her reasons for doing so a matter of conjecture. We can suppose that it came through frustration of her hopes for marriage with Cepeda. A poem which she wrote to Sabater, in effect accepting his suit, makes it clear that what she feels for her future husband is affection and compassion, rather than love.

Pedro Sabater, like the other men in Tula's life, was a bit younger than she. He had had a surprisingly distinguished career by the time of the marriage. At the age of thirty he was a deputy to the *Cortes* (the equivalent of a congressmen), and had been named civil governor of Madrid and its province. From Valencia,

Sabater had written a successfully produced play, and like Tassara, courted his future wife in poetry. He was also seriously ill, as Tula was aware when the wedding took place. Sabater seems to have had cancer of the larynx. The couple was married on May 10, 1846, and left within a few days for Paris where Sabater was to undergo a tracheotomy. The operation was unsuccessful, and he died in Bordeaux on August 1, 1846. The marriage had lasted less than four months, and the loss of the husband for whom she had acquired a deep affection grieved la Avellaneda profoundly. She did not return to Spain until November, temporarily entering a convent in Bordeaux where she passed her time in prayer, meditation, and the writing of a *Devocionario* ("prayer book") in both prose and verse, which was published many years afterward. While the real-life drama was being played out in Paris, one of Tula's plays was produced in Madrid. Entitled *Egilona*, this effort did not achieve the success of the earlier dramas.

X   *The Widow in Madrid*

By early 1847, the letters to Cepeda have resumed. Tula speaks of having aged and having lost her inspiration and desire to write, but also tells the former lover of a new aspirant for her hand, whom she had refused. Cepeda arrived in Madrid in September, but there are eleven more letters written to him, even when the two were seeing each other almost daily. She is afraid to love him, she writes, and yet cannot bear not to see him. Tula is living once again the drama of a hopeless love. In the decade since the relationship began in Seville, the volatile Gertrudis had not changed. Nor had Cepeda, who ran away from her once again. She had finally to resign herself, not without great pain and difficulty. She went, as on the death of her husband, to a convent where, through meditation and prayer, she sought expiation. She also wrote a lengthy poem to Cepeda that begins: "No existe lazo ya; todo está roto: / plúgole al cielo así: ¡bendito sea!" ("There exist no bonds now; all is reft: / blessed be the heaven that has so resolved!").[22] What writing la Avellaneda did in this period is primarily of a religious nature, a characteristic of hers in periods of depression.

Not until June of 1849 did a new nonreligious work appear. A long short story or novelette entitled *La velada del helecho, o el donativo del diablo* (*The Vigil of the Fern Plant, or The Gift of the Devil*), it was based on a Swiss folktale that Tula's brother Manuel had recounted to her. Three years after its publication in novel form, it was produced on the stage as a drama under the title of *El donativo del diablo* (*The Gift of the Devil*). The period of crisis over, la Avellaneda spent part of the summer at the Escorial and at La Granja de San Ildefonso, taking an active part in the social activities of the court circles in both places. The fall of the same year saw another triumph in the theater. In 1844, five years before the opening, she had written a biblical drama based on the Book of Kings that she entitled *Saúl.* She had read it to members of the *Liceo* of Madrid and she had shown it to French friends and authors during the ill-fated trip to Paris with her husband Sabater. At a sumptuous opening attended by the royal family as well as the major figures of the literary world, Tula was once again honored publicly. The play did not have a long run, but enjoyed a great critical and literary success.

The major literary accomplishment of la Avellaneda in the following year was the issuance of a second volume of poetry, including poems already published in the collection of 1841, a portrait of the author, a dedication to the queen, and fifty-four new poems. Not merely the poet, the playwright and novelist were also at work. Tula wrote that the censorship had approved a new drama which she had written entitled *Recaredo.* She appears to have been concurrently preparing two prose works, one, a novel entitled *Dolores,* and the other, *La ondina del lago azul o los merodeadores del siglo XV* (*The Water Sprite of the Blue Lake or the Marauders of the Fifteenth Century*).[23] In 1850, at the opening of the new Teatro Real (Royal Theater) in Madrid, a poem of La Avellaneda was read along with contributions by other major poets of the period, and at about the same time, there appeared in a Madrid periodical, *La Ilustración,* an autobiographical statement that is important in its portrayal of the author as she saw herself. Here Tula confesses that her youthful character was marked by impetuousness, violent reactions, and a determination to have her own way. She mentions remarks that her talent was of the strength of a man's rather than a woman's, but protests, interestingly enough, that, "no man sees certain things in the way that I see them."[24] She recognizes also what the love affair with Cepeda has done to her emotionally, without naming him, of course, but now that we have her letters to him, we can relate her statements concerning her loss of energy to that. "At the present time," she writes, "my character is broken; I am less irritable, and I have lost the enthusiasm that was its base."

Dolores appeared during 1851 in the *Semanario Pintoresco* in serial form. Shortly after, the same magazine issued a legend of la Avellaneda entitled *La montaña maldita: Tradición suiza* (*The Accursed Mountain: Swiss Tradition*). In October, the play *Recaredo*, written two years earlier but not accepted by the censorship, was finally produced. The royal family attended the opening night, and the critics were again full of praise, comparing the three-act tragedy to *Munio Alfonso* and to *Saúl*. Adverse criticism was also heard but did not deter the author from pursuing her writing of drama at an intensive pace. During the single year of 1852 la Avellaneda saw five dramatic works produced, of which four were full-length works of three acts each. The first, *La verdad vence apariencias* (*Truth Conquers Appearances*), had been finished by December of 1851, at which time Tula gave a successful reading before a group of literary friends. Next followed a production of a straight play in prose, *Errores del corazón* (*Errors of the Heart*), with which la Avellaneda triumphed once again. The third play was based on the legend published earlier as *La velada del helecho* (*The Vigil of the Fern Plant*). For the drama, Tula utilized only the second half of the title: *El donativo del diablo* (*The Gift of the Devil*). The critics reacted badly, and soon the play closed. Later the same month, however, another work opened to an immediate and resounding success. This was *La hija de las flores* (*The Daughter of the Flowers*). A contemporary newspaper account states that there had been few triumphs in the Spanish theater to equal it. Laurel wreaths and flowers were thrown on the stage as the authoress was applauded by the audience.[25] The fifth dramatic work was one in which la Avellaneda collaborated with several other writers, a panegyric or *loa* entitled *El héroe de Bailén* (*The Hero of Bailen*) and composed in posthumous honor of a general.

Tula had become a major figure in the world of the theater as well as of poetry.

XI *The Affair of the Academy*

It is not surprising, then, that she aspired to the chair of the Royal Spanish Academy left vacant by the death of Juan Nicasio Gallego in January of 1853. There was something of a precedent for naming a woman to the Academy. One, a sixteen-year-old daughter of a nobleman, had received a sort of honorary appointment at the insistence of King Charles III in the late eighteenth century. However, La Avellaneda was not a candidate for an honorary position, but for an appointment in the fullest sense. Whether Gallego wished for his friend Tula to succeed him, as she was to assert, or not, is not to the point, nor was the affirmation effective in her pursuit of the seat. No one doubted or questioned the applicant's talents and important literary accomplishments. On the basis of merit, Gertrudis was a very strong candidate, but it was not on that basis that the decision was made. The academicians were to vote on the proposition "¿Son admisibles o no las señoras a plazas de número de la Academia?" ("Are women admissible or are they not, to the seats on the Academy?"). The final vote was six members favoring the admission of women, and fourteen against. Passions concerning the affair ran high, and Tula herself accused another candidate, the powerful political figure don Luis José Sartorius, count of San Luis, of duplicity in the matter. When the latter officially withdrew his own candidacy, the Academy elected the relatively unknown Antonio Ferrer del Río. This body did send la Avellaneda a letter praising her talents and accomplishments and assuring her of the esteem in which they held the author of *Munio Alfonso, Saul* and *The Daughter of the Flowers*. Nevertheless, the wounds were deep. La Avellaneda was to write bitterly about it later, and her enemies were implacable in their assaults. She was dubbed "Doña Safo" or "Lady Sappho" by one group that attacked her.[26]

Despite this, however, Tula's work went on. The play that she adapted from the French, *La aventurera* (*The Adventuress*), scored another major success on the stage. Eight days after the opening of the former there followed another work adapted from the French entitled *Hortensia,* which met with less success. Shortly thereafter, also without success, came still another work entitled *La sonámbula (The Sleepwalker).* The public disappointments that these failures represent were paralleled in la Avellaneda's personal life. In March of 1854 she wrote to Cepeda that tragedy had struck her family. The death of her sister, leaving three small children, had devastated her mother, for whom she herself was caring.[27] The responsibilities that this brought to her, plus her own state of neurasthenia and despair, had prevented any creative writing. She had bought a country house in the hopes of retiring to it, she wrote, to remove herself from the pressures and the malevolence of the capital, as well as for reasons of health. The collapse of her mother made it imperative for her to return to Madrid. She contemplated entering a convent or returning to America if her mother died. Pessimism and bitterness set the tone of the letters. The final catastrophe came with the news that Cepeda had married another woman. She had lost him finally and irrevocably.

As in earlier years, she took refuge in her work. By early 1855, she had presented three new plays, two short ones and one fulllength one for production. The two one-act plays were entitled *Simpatía y antipatía (Amity and Aversion)* and *La hija del rey René (The Daughter of King René).* The five-act drama was entitled *Oráculos de Talía o los duendes en palacio (Oracles of Thalia or The Ghosts in the Palace).* The latter, while neither as successful nor as impressive as other works of la Avellaneda, is interesting for its comments on the problems of the person with artistic talent and bent, reflecting the disillusionment of the author in many passages. Critics of the play were to provide her with even more disappointment, with the result that she determined not to write for the stage again, a resolution to which she held for some three years.

In March, 1855, Tula was invited to participate in the public crowning of the aged poet Manuel José Quintana, an impressive public affair at which the queen herself placed the poet's crown upon his head. La Avellaneda wrote the ode which begins "Allá, en el centro de la hermosa Antilla, / que oye bramar al golfo mejicano; / perla que a la corona de Castilla / aun rinde el mundo de Colón ufano..." ("There in the center of the beautiful Antilles, / that harkens to the roar of Mexico's gulf; / pearl that Columbus's world still proffers / proudly to Castilla's crown..."). She read the poem herself to the assembled dignitaries, and appears in the painting commemorating the event with the manuscript in hand. While still an impressive woman in the portrait, she is already corpulent and assuming the matronly look of her later portraits.[28]

XII Marriage to Verdugo

Just over forty, Avellaneda survived several youthful engagements, the lengthy and painful involvement with Cepeda, the brief but disastrous love affair with Tassara, and the loss of their daughter and of her husband, but her life of the heart was not yet over. Some time in 1855, probably after the July revolution and the fall from power of the count of San Luis, she met artillery colonel don Domingo Verdugo y Massieu. He was a close associate of General O'Donnell, the head of the Liberal party to which la Avellaneda had decided to give her allegiance. Verdugo, like Tula's other lovers, was younger than she by three years. A prominent figure by the time the couple met, he had been named aide to the king and a gentleman of the chamber. Consequently, when the two decided to wed, the ceremony took place in the Royal Palace on April 26, 1855, and the monarchs, through the marquises of Santa Cruz de Mudela, were their witnesses. Excepting several poems, little appeared from the pen of the new bride during more than two years. Not until the death of Quintana in 1857 did she once more read a poem in the company of the same literary figures that had praised and honored him two years earlier.

Her literary output resumed with the publication of poems in various periodicals of the period, *La América, El Correo de la Moda*, and in collections such as the *Album de la Zarzuela*. More significant, however, was la Avellaneda's decision to take up her role as playwright once again. On March 20, 1858, her drama *Los tres amores (Three Loves)* opened in the Teatro del Circo. The theme of three types of love, embodied in the three leading characters, a woman and the two men who are in love with her, has overtones of autobiographical experience that the Madrid audience could not have recognized, but which add to the interest for anyone studying Tula's drama. The opening was not, however, a success. Hostility by the critics had silenced the author's pen for some three years, and that same hostility assumed a public and cruel form during the opening night performance. Noticeable unrest in one section of the theater became louder and louder as the production went on. Finally as a secondary character, the marquise, spoke the line which is the equivalent of the English proverb "Something's rotten in Denmark"—"hay gato en cerrado" ("There's a cat locked up in here")—a live cat was thrown on the stage by one of the men in the orchestra box who had been creating the disturbances. Even the presence of the king and queen in the opening-night audience could not prevent the inevitable laughter and ensuing uproar. The repercussions and events growing out of the incident were to have a lasting effect on Tula's life and work. In the meantime, however, a second work opened that was to be a theatrical and literary triumph. The second great biblical drama of la Avellaneda, it was entitled *Baltasar*. The opening on April 9, 1858, was a brilliant success with both critics and audience. But La Avellaneda's moment of triumph was very short-lived.

XIII   The "Stabbing Incident"

Five days after the opening of *Baltasar* and just less than three weeks after the scandalous interruption of *Three Loves*, la Avellaneda's husband, Colonel Verdugo, was stabbed and very seriously wounded in a street incident that has never been fully explained.[29] So grave was the stilleto wound that Verdugo was carried to the nearby house of a friend and there administered extreme unction. The man who had attacked him was one Antonio Ribera, who had been in exile in London for his libelous attacks on General O'Donnell, with whom Verdugo was closely associated politically. Apparently Ribera was the instigator of the "cat incident" in the theater, and Verdugo had made an insulting remark to the man concerning his actions. To what extent there was also a political motive in the stabbing was never established, although, given the prominence of both Verdugo and his wife, the press published lengthy and frequent articles about the occurrence. To further complicate the matter, la Avellaneda herself, three days after the event, wrote a letter to the queen which was published in *La América* and then quickly withdrawn. In that letter, subsequent accounts indicate, the overwrought wife ascribed political motives to the would-be killer and categorized it as a political crime. Despite the doctors' fears, Verdugo did not die, but his recovery was never complete. It was Tula's destiny once again to nurse an ailing husband.

Once Verdugo's health permitted, the couple left Madrid for a lengthy trip through the north of Spain, parts of France, and later to Barcelona and Valencia. Tula kept a diary and took extensive travel notes, as well as collecting several legends which she wrote up and subsequently published. After his treatment in southern France, Verdugo and Tula reentered Spain via the Mediterranean coast, arriving in Barcelona during October of 1858. Verdugo had close friends in Barcelona, and the couple was warmly received. La Avellaneda was feted at public festivities in her honor. *The Daughter of the Flowers* was given a special performance as a part of the homage to the author. In November another performance of the same play was given, and the author honored by a second literary group. Later, in Valencia, the honors continued, although Tula herself wrote to friends that the delicate state of her husband's health had made her stop work on the poem "Al árbol de Guernica" ("To the Tree of Guernica") begun earlier in their trip.

Not until the rigors of winter were over did the Verdugos return to Madrid. During the summer of 1859, they again went to northern Spain, passing through Durango and Guernica, and visiting Bayonne and Biarritz in France. They traveled to Lourdes and then to Cauterets to take the medicinal waters. La Avellaneda managed to gather more legendary material, the result of which was a legend entitled *La ondina del lago azul* (*The Water Sprite of the Blue Lake*). The story is one that reappears in literature, that of the dreamy youth who falls in love with a vision of beauty formed from the illusion of moonlight and the mist that rises from the lake. He finally commits suicide, throwing himself into the waters that he believes enclose the woman that is his ideal. The most famous version of the tale in Spanish, of course, is Gustavo Adolfo Bécquer's *Los ojos verdes* (*The Green Eyes*).

XIV   *The Return to Cuba*

Shortly after the return of Gertrudis and her husband to Madrid, don Francisco Serrano, duke de la Torre, was named captain-general of Cuba. He was a close friend of Verdugo, and his wife, like Gertrudis, had been born in Cuba. Serrano was governor from 1859 to 1862 and brought about many beneficial reforms during his stay in office. He invited Verdugo to come with him, and the two couples embarked on a battleship, landing in Cuba on November 24, 1859. Tula had had to leave a dying mother, but was back in the homeland that she had left twenty-four years before. Hardly had they arrived when the festivities and public homages to la Avellaneda began, continuing for much of the five years of her stay in Cuba.

Tula for her part made various contributions to these public occasions, writing poems to fit the many festivities in her honor, among them a companion piece to the early sonnet composed in 1836 as she departed her native shores. She entitled it "La vuelta a la patria" ("The Return to the Homeland"). Her engraved portrait was passed out and numerous laudatory verses were read at entertainments to welcome her. In early December a musical evening was prepared for her in Havana, and during the Christmas holidays extravagant parties were held. The most important function, however, took place at the end of January, 1860, in the Teatro Tacón of Havana. This was the public ceremony of crowning the poetess with a golden wreath made especially for the occasion. Medals of commemoration were struck in gold, silver, and bronze. There was a concert, a performance of Tula's play *La hija del rey René* (*The Daughter of King René*), and finally the crowning of la Avellaneda. Poems and speeches to the author were made, and Gertrudis replied with a poem. A special coach took her home after the ceremony.[30]

Shortly afterward, Colonel Verdugo was named governor of the province of Cienfuegos. Tula stayed on in Havana for several days preparing publication of a magazine which she edited for some six months, and in which she published various articles and stories, some of them previously published in Spain and some of them original. The magazine, entitled the *Album Cubano*, appeared twice a month for twelve issues.[31] Among other things that she wrote for it, Tula prepared a biography of the poetess Sappho in which she makes rather obvious references, not to the life of the ancient Greek writer, but to episodes in her own experience. She also published articles in which she set out to demonstrate the intellectual quality of women and the moral superiority of women over men, utilizing the names of various celebrated women of history to make her point concerning women's abilities.

In Cienfuegos with her husband, Gertrudis was welcomed with a special concert in her honor, as was done when she made her only visit to her home town of Puerto Príncipe in May, 1860. The Philharmonic Society organized an evening of music and poetry honoring the famous native daughter. The concert hall was decorated with the titles of la Avellaneda's works in letters of gold and a large portrait of the artist herself.

Before leaving the governorship of Cienfuegos, Verdugo and Gertrudis saw the inauguration of a new theater which was duly named Teatro de la Avellaneda. Verdugo fell ill of yellow fever which further undermined his precarious state of health, but recovered sufficiently to assume the governorship of Cárdenas, a post which he held from August, 1860, until September, 1863. Letters to friends written during this period indicate that Gertrudis was not well herself. Suffering from the intense heat of Cuba to which she no longer was accustomed, she experienced attacks of nerves, severe headaches, and even convulsions.[32] Despite this, she continued to work with the indomitable determination shown in earlier years when the passion of love tortured her head, and her spirit still sustained her. In addition to the magazine she edited in Havana, she wrote a novel entitled *El artista barquero o los cuatro cinco de junio* (*The Boatman Artist or the Four June Fifths*), published in 1861, and set in France during the reign of Louis XV. She also completed two legends based on American themes, *El aura blanca* (*The White Vulture*), set in Puerto Príncipe, and *El cacique de Tumerqúe* (*The Cacique of Tumerqúe*), a tale of the sixteenth century in the viceroyship of New Granada.

More public ceremonies were held in Tula's honor. The city of Matanzas had invited her to the opening of their *Liceo* in 1859, but the invitation came just as Gertrudis had learned of the death of her mother in Madrid. Two years later, another invitation was made, this time to participate in a charity bazaar in early November, 1861. La Avellaneda made a donation of an album beginning with a poem "To Matanzas." During the four days of the Bazaar, continuous festivities centered primarily on Gertrudis. On the last day, the poetess was again honored with a crown made of laurel and gold.

In Cárdenas, Tula wrote poems for the unveiling of a new statue to Christopher Columbus, one of which was set to music and performed at the ceremonies. She also wrote such poems as "Al pendón de Castilla" ("To the Flag of Castille"), which commemorates the entry of Spanish troops in Tetuán in northern Morocco, a light and lilting *Serenata* (*Serenade*) written for a friend, and "A un cocuyo" ("To a Firefly").

XV   The Second Widowhood

Events were also occuring in her personal life which deeply affected Tula. Her brother Manuel had married a wealthy Cuban of French descent, and at the insistence of his wife, Manuel left Cuba for residence in Paris. Colonel Verdugo was transferred to Pinar del Río as lieutenant governor, but shortly after taking up his new post, he fell ill with fever and died on October 28, 1863, at the age of forty-six. His death affected Gertrudis deeply. She prepared a will, gave her gold crown to the Church of Our Lady of Bethlehem in Havana, and during the winter of 1864 began preparations to enter a convent. Only the arrival of her brother Manuel in the spring prevented her from doing so. On May 21, she set sail from Cuba for the last time, going to New York for a visit to the United States where she, like Heredia before her, visited and wrote a poem on Niagara Falls. After a stay of two months, she left for Europe, going first to London and then to Paris before returning to Spain. She decided to settle in Seville, where she lived for four years, becoming a friend of the novelist, Cecilia Böhl de Faber, whose works appeared under the pseudonym of Fernán Caballero, and who nicknamed her "Gertrudis la Magna."

The most important literary undertaking of this dispirited and somber final period of la Avellaneda's life was the preparation of her complete works, published over a period of three years, 1869 to 1871, in five large volumes, one of poetry, two of the dramas, and two of the novels and other works in prose. Hardly any of the works were left unaltered, and critics have frequently expressed their disapproval of the changes that la Avellaneda made. In addition, Tula wrote two new plays, one a version of a French play by Alexandre Dumas and Auguste Maquet entitled *Catalina*. The other was a farce called *El millonario y la maleta* (*The Millionaire and the Suitcase*). Neither play was produced. She also undertook the rewriting of the prayer book begun in Bordeaux on the death of her first husband, which had been lost.

In 1867, Tula journeyed first to Madrid and then to Paris to visit her brother Manuel. It was at this time that she sent a lengthy letter protesting her love of her native country. Unpleasant attacks, alleging that she had abandoned Cuba, had hurt her deeply, and she replied in her own defense.

The revolution of 1868 that resulted in the loss of the throne for Isabel II, could not have done other than affect her also. She had long been closely associated with the royal family, and the queen had repeatedly shown her marked signs of deference. While she considered moving permanently to Paris, her brother Manuel died suddenly, and the loss for the sister who had been so close to him was great. His widow came to Spain and lived for some time with la Avellaneda after the latter had moved once more to Madrid, in 1870.

Tula's health was poor by this time. She was diabetic, and the political situation of Spain combined with her brother's death hastened her decline. In 1872, she rewrote her will and, on February 1, 1873, she died at the age of fifty-six. Of the several literary figures present at the funeral, only don Juan Valera's name has any meaning to us today. She was first buried in Madrid; later her remains were transferred to Seville to the Cemetery of San Fernando. The centenary of Tula's birth, in

1914, was marked by extensive ceremonies at the University of Havana with speeches and scholarly studies of La Avellaneda's works. Most importantly, her complete works, plus some of the dramas not originally included, were reissued in six volumes.

CHAPTER 2

The Lyric Poetry

G ERTRUDIS Gómez de Avellaneda was first and foremost
a poet. Whatever negative criticism may have been leveled
at certain of her dramas or her novels, the praise for her poetry
was consistently high. Contemporary critics as well as recent
ones have repeatedly spoken of her genius as fundamentally
lyrical. Furthermore, her place in the annals of Spanish literature has survived mainly through her poems. Histories and
anthologies that barely mention her other accomplishments
acknowledge her skill and success as a poetess. Her control
and mastery of meter and rhyme was brilliant, and her output,
once one considers the plays written entirely in verse form as
well as the published lyric poetry, is impressive in quantity as
well as in quality.

Tula's undeniable gift for poetry became apparent at a very
early age. Her autobiographical writings tell us that she was
already writing verses at the age of nine, having composed
poems on the death of her father at that time. She continued to
write poetry through her adolescence in Cuba, although to
what extent that poetry survived or was incorporated into the
later volumes of published poems is something that we do not
know. If we accept the date which Tula herself assigned to her
poems—and we know that her dating was frequently inac-
curate—then the bulk of these youthful works have not survived.
The first extant poem that can be dated exactly is the frequently
reproduced "Al partir" ("On Leaving"), written when Gertrudis
was twenty-two years old.

By the time she reached Seville in 1838, writing had become
more than a youthful avocation. She did publish poems and
translations under the pen name of "La Peregrina" and was

49

known locally, but we cannot say that Tula's true literary career began until she reached Madrid at the age of twenty-six. The reading of her poetry at a meeting of the *Liceo* of Madrid in 1840 by the famous José Zorrilla marks the entry of la Avelleneda into the literary world of her day. From that time on, Tula's poems were solicited in the highest literary and social circles, read, applauded, and praised. Her first volume of poems, which contained fifty-four pieces, appeared in 1841, a few short months after her arrival in the capital. A second volume comprising one hundred and twenty-nine poems of varying lengths, was published in 1850, and reissued both in the first volume of the *Obras completas* (*Complete Works*) in 1869, and in the centennial edition of 1914.

The total poetic output of la Avellaneda might be said to constitute a sort of compendium or panorama of styles in Hispanic poetry from late neoclassicism through romanticism. Versatile Tula tried her hand at the various prevailing fashions in poetry, and was eminently successful in her attempts. The influences on her work, rich and varied, include major French and English poets as well as Spanish and Latin American. Her early acquisition of French enabled her to read the works of Lamartine and Victor Hugo in the original, and of Byron in translation. The Spaniards Meléndez Valdés and Quintana and the Cuban poet Heredia exercised a lasting effect on her poetry and her thinking. In Madrid, Tula was in close contact with most of the major—and the minor—literary figures of her time, including Quintana, Lista, Espronceda, Zorrilla, Pastor Díaz, Nicasio Gallego, and Juan Valera, to name the best known.

Highly praised by these men, she was considered their creative equal. They spoke of her, whether rightly or wrongly, as the greatest woman poet of all Hispanic literature. She was once ranked above Sor Juana Inés de la Cruz, with whom it would be natural to compare her, and considered far superior to any of the female "amateurs" who had dabbled in verse during the Golden Age. Whether to rank her as highly today—or even above her own contemporaries, Carolina Coronado and Rosalía de Castro—is another matter. What was greatly admired by her peers in her own time is not necessarily attractive to us today. Aesthetics have changed. Our literary outlook is quite different from that of the mid-nineteenth century, the period of her most striking triumphs. Even before her death in 1873, important changes were taking place in the concepts of what truly constituted poetry and what was better suited to prose. For this reason it is particularly difficult to classify la Avellaneda's poetry as simply or fully romantic in the sense that we may with the work of an Espronceda in Spanish or a Keats or Shelley in English.

By the time Gertrudis arrived in Madrid in 1840, the brief period of romantic intensity and novelty was already waning. Larra was dead, and Espronceda was soon to die. The "revolution," if romanticism's advent can be termed that in Spain, had replaced a neoclassicism imported from France that the Spanish public—except for a small elite—had never readily accepted. As romanticism settled into socially, politically, and religiously acceptable chanels, it rapidly became the norm for literary expression. A "second generation" then established itself, and the rebellious intensity of the first romantics entered a more conventional and prosaic phase. Romanticism was already becoming ossified in some aspects of form and content by the time of La Avellaneda's arrival in Madrid. Consequently, any approach to her poetry, or appraisal of it, must take into consideration the changing aesthetics. Even the word "lyrical" as applied to poetry has changed and has a sense today that is far more restricted than in the 1840s and 1850s.

What we shall be considering here are the poems which Tula herself included in her two volumes of "poesía lírica," excluding passages—often beautifully lyrical—of the verse dramas. The richness of thematic development and her use of the whole range of metrical and rhyme possibilities of Spanish poetry attest to the virtuosity of the poetess and her mastery of technique.

As the facts of la Avellaneda's life clearly shows us, the woman herself is an embodiment of romanticism. Her rebellious spirit from childhood on, her lack of conventionality and liberty of conduct in such matters as her love affair with Tassara, her independence and willfulness in a male-dominated social and literary world, her sense of loneliness and of exile from her homeland and the society in which she lived, her sensitivity to nature, her bouts with melancholy and depression, her identification with lonely individuals and "wanderers," her protracted pursuit of a great and ill-fated love, the moments of ecstasy and exultation followed by the aftermath of disillusion and torment, all are things which we associate with the romantic psyche, and all of these elements are present in varying degrees in her poetry.

Thematically, her poetic production is usually divided into several categories, but any such classification must necessarily run afoul of the problem of themes that are developed within poems but which are not central to the corpus of her work. Categorization by theme is consequently artificial. It is, however, helpful in providing an approach to a study of la Avellaneda's poetry. The themes include: Cuba, love and eroticism, poetry itself, neoclassical motifs, Spain, religion, philosophical meditations, personal and public occasions, and poetic portraits. In the best poems or passages thereof, we sense the authentic voice of Gertrudis, but even in her less successful moments, her skill in the handling of prevailing forms and poetic fashions is always striking.

I *The Theme of Cuba*

The earliest poem of la Avellaneda, as previously mentioned, is also one of her best known and most frequently reprinted. Entitled "Al partir" ("On Leaving"), it was written in 1836 when the poetess was twenty-two, at the time of departure from Havana for Europe. It is a sonnet, and both the precision of its form and the lyrical evocation of its content may be considered characteristic of Tula's poetic talents.

The theme of the poem, one which persists throughout la Avellaneda's poetry, is Cuba, and the love for the homeland which she would not see again for over two decades. The first lines evoke the island with the exclamatory "¡Perla del mar! ¡Estrella de Occidente!" and then "¡Hermosa Cuba!" The tone is evocatory with a note of exaltation, as is the following phrase, "tu brillante cielo" ("thy brilliant sky"), but almost immediately the note of pain and sadness is introduced. It is then that the exclamatory phrases of the opening can be seen as the author's

cry of anguish on leaving the land of her birth. The night's dark
well parallels the author's growing emotion as the ship's crew
prepares for sailing. To this is added the somber note of terror
and uncertainty in the future, "el hado en su furor" ("fate in
its fury"), the almost elegiac tone of the two "adiós," and then
the closing lines of the second tercet describing the tranquil
departure of the ship with its sharp contrast to the inner turmoil
and drama of the poetess herself. Whether as foreboding or
through a sense of premonition, Tula was embarking on the sea
of life as well. She perceived, along with the mystique of Cuba
and of nature, a mystique of self, that she was setting out on a
pilgrimage that would make of her a wanderer or "peregrina"
as she would characterize herself via her pseudonym at the
beginning of her literary career in Spain.

Al partir

¡Perla del mar! ¡Estrella de Occidente!
¡Hermosa Cuba! Tu brillante cielo
la noche cubre con su opaco velo,
como cubre el dolor mi triste frente.

¡Voy a partir! . . . La chusma diligente,
para arrancarme del nativo suelo
las velas iza, y pronta a su desvelo
la brisa acude de tu zona ardiente.

¡Adiós, patria feliz, edén querido!
¡Doquier que el hado en su furor me impela,
tu dulce nombre halagará mi oído!

¡Adiós! . . . Ya cruje la turgente vela . . .
El ancla se alza . . . el buque, estremecido,
¡las alas corta y silencioso vuela!

(*OB* I, 237)

On Leaving

Pearl of the sea! Star of the Occident!
Beautiful Cuba! Night's murky veil
Is drawn across the sky's refulgent trail,
And I succumb to sorrow's ravishment.

Now I depart! . . . As to their labors bent,
The crewmen now their tasks assail,
To wrest me from my home, they hoist the sail
To catch the ardent winds that you have sent.

Farewell, my Eden, land so dear!
Whatever in its furor fate now sends,
Your cherished name will grace my ear!

Farewell! . . . The anchor from the sea ascends,
The sails are full. . . . The ship breaks clear,
And with soft quiet motion, wave and water fends.

The companion poem, "La vuelta a la patria" ("The Return
to the Homeland"), which la Avellaneda wrote more than
twenty years later on her return to Cuba begins with the same
evocatory phrase: "¡Perla del mar!" The tone and development
of the latter work are quite different from those of "Al partir,"
although similarities can be found as well. She again calls the
island "hermosa Cuba" and the "tranquilo edén de mi infancia"
("tranquil eden of my youth"), the "tierra bendita" ("blessed
land") of "brisas perfumadas" ("perfumed breezes"), she speaks
of the exotic flora and fauna of Cuba, the mockingbird, the
seiba tree, the orange tree and the pineapple, the coffee tree,
of the vast savannahs, the jungles, the mountains, and of the
tropical sun. The result is a moving poem radiating sincerity
and the depth of Tula's feeling for the country from which she
had been absent for so long. The total effect of the poem, however, is one of nostalgia, as though its author recognized that
the past could not be relived or recaptured. She describes
herself as having a "con el semblante marchito / por el tiempo
y la desgracia" ("face that has been wizened by time and misfortune"), (OB I, 339–340). Fate in its furor had dealt with her
harshly in her personal life. The energies and hopes of a healthy
young woman, determined to see and conquer a world, were
not what they had been two decades before. Tula describes,
she praises, she expresses her feelings, but the rhetorical phrases
interspersed throughout make this poem not only much longer
than its companion piece, but quite different. The freshness
and relative simplicity of "Al partir" are gone, as is its succinct-
ness.

Nevertheless, the later poem offers evidence that la Avellaneda's poetic talent had not been fully mined out. Even when not responding to such deeply felt or moving sentiments while writing such poems—almost mere exercises in verse—as "A las cubanas" ("To Cuban Women"), (*OB* I, 340–341). "A un cocuyo" ("To a Firefly"), (*OB* I, 342–343), or "El viajero americano" ("The American Traveler"), (*OB* I, 302), she achieves descriptive passages of beauty and a verbal skill that is still impressive. Portions of her "Serenata de Cuba" (Cuban Serenade"), (*OB* I, 348–350), written for the birthday celebration of Tula's friend the duchess de la Torre, foreshadow in elegance of imagery and language the Watteauesque poems of Rubén Darío at the end of the century. The poem begins with the voice of the poet:

> ¡Oh Antilla dichosa! ¿Qué mágicos sones,
> que luz inefable, que extraña alegría,
> del cielo destierran los negros crespones,
> prestando a esta noche la pompa del día?

> Oh fortunate Antilles! what magical sounds,
> What ineffable glow, what unusual delight,
> Banish the evening's dark velvety bounds,
> Granting the pomp of the day to deepening night?

> (*OB* I, 348)

In this magical night of moonlight, perfumed breezes, and the soft sound of running brooks, the palm trees sigh and the fireflies flit through the trees like stars. In a magical moment of harmony, each voice of nature speaks, the stars, the flowers, drops of dew, birds, the breeze, and so on. Less rhetorical than much other poetry written for specific occasions, this work's interest lies in its simplicity and minor tone as well as its imagery and language.

II *The Theme of Love*

One of the fundamental themes of la Avellaneda's poetry is love. As we know from Tula's biography, Eros played a central role in many events of her life. Love is a major theme also of her dramas, her novels, and her other prose writing. The letters to Cepeda have been published as *Cartas de amor* or *Cartas amorosas*,[1] and the titles are apt, as these epistles are, in every sense, "love letters." At least two of la Avellaneda's best-known poems were written to Cepeda and express in compressed and poetic form the trajectory that the love affair takes in the more extensive letters. Both poems are entitled simply "A él" ("To Him"), the "him" of the titles being, of course, Ignacio de Cepeda. As we have noted; both of the poetess's marriages followed breaks with Cepeda, the first marriage to Sabater in 1846, and the second marriage to Verdugo in 1855, after Cepeda himself had married and her hopes for her own future with him had been dashed. The second of the two poems clearly refers to the final break, offering the epitaph of love, while the earlier poem is still full of hope, a shadowed and already somber hope, but not yet resignation.

The first poem, considerably longer and more complex in meter and structure than the later one, consists of twenty-two stanzas. The first twelve, in octosyllablic verse, have a rhyme scheme of *a b a a b c d c c d*, and so on. The thirteenth stanza, while keeping the same verse length, alters the rhyme scheme to *y z z y z*, the first and third lines ending in *verso agudo* ("aquel" and "El") rather than the *verso llano* of the previous stanzas. The last nine stanzas, of four dodecasyllabic lines each, are rhymed *a b a b, c d c d* to the end. These metric divisions indicate the three major parts of the thematic developments of the poem; a fourth change of tone and concept comes in the last four stanzas.

The first portion describes the unspoiled world of the poetess's adolescence, when she had begun to dream of love, but had not yet known love's reality. She is still in the Arcadia of innocence in which the mind can conjure up images of the enchanted ideal being one hopes to find. The concept, of course, is a fairly common one in the romantic canon, and we can assume that its usage here results both from artistic convention as well as being based on experience. In her autobiography of 1850, la Avellaneda had written of herself: "I had a world inside my head that was not a real world. Life and people did not correspond to what I had imagined. I began to suffer."[2] Certainly this was

the case in her love for Cepeda, but the description of the poem
gives us a portrait, in the early stanzas, of the "world inside the
head" as yet unsullied. The poem begins as follows:

> En la aurora lisonjera
> de mi juventud florida,
> en aquella edad primera
> —Breve y dulce primavera,
> de tantas flores vestida—

> In lifetime's transient, jocund dawn,
> youth's precious moment quickly checked,
> in that first age too soon withdrawn,
> brief, dulcet spring so swiftly gone,
> with flowers festively bedecked.

(OB I, 253)

In this paradise of youth, the poetess's soul "full of mystical
enchantment," listened to the whispers of love that all nature
around her provided. She understood that "her heart / was
calling to an ideal being." Suddenly she saw in her mind's eye
the ardent and living being that was her dream, his head held
high, his voice full of "sweetness strange." Who, she asks her
soul, is that "beloved phantasm," who has no name? ¿Un genio?
¿Un ángel? ¿Un hombre?" ("A spirit? An Angel? A man?").
The answer quickly follows: "¡Ah, lo sabes! era El" ("Oh, you
know that it was He!").

Finally the hour of meeting came. Tula's heart responded:
"Porque era, no hay duda, tu imagen querida, / que el alma
inspirada logró adivinar" (Because it was, there was no doubt,
your winsome face / my soul's deep inspiration had divined"),
(OB I, 253). The felicity, however, was soon marred. Even though
the poetess had seen her "Northern star," all was not innocence
and beauty in her garden of life. She speaks of the serpent
from her native land that has the power of making a sound that
hypnotizes birds and makes them fall, and of the gentle butterfly caught in the flame or the water of the spring that is swallowed
up in the sea. Then she asks if indeed this lover will be her
flame, her sea, her serpent. It does not matter ("¿Qué importa?"),
for her heart accepts and loves. She is like the leaf that powerful

winds carry away ("la hoja que el viento potente arrebata"). Besides the theme of childhood and innocence lost, appears the development of the motif of the satanic figure that ensnares his victim in the nets of erotic love. The Cepeda of the poem is not the angelic figure of the youthful vision, but the fallen angel whose power is ultimately evil and maleficent. The poem implies, as do la Avellaneda's letters, that her lover was a heartless man, a *bel homme sans merci* rather than the traditional *belle dame*, who holds Keat's wretched youth in thrall.

The second poem to Cepeda, seven stanzas long, is less complex but rings truer. The image of the avenging angel is the only one that la Avellaneda employs: "¡Angel de las venganzas! ya eres hombre..." ("Avenging angel! You are a man..."), (*OB* I, 297). Nevertheless, the reinforcement of this image by other passages of the poem make it a powerful and central one. The spell has been broken, however. The question of the previous poem has been answered. The lover is neither spirit nor angel: he is a man. The eternal love, the unquestioning love, the "leaf" that is carried wherever the winds of Eros take it, is over: "No existen lazos ya: todo está roto" ("There exist no bonds now; all is reft"). The note of religiosity that follows— "plúgolo al cielo así: ¡bendito sea!" ("Blessed be the heaven that has so resolved")—fits into the pattern that the poetess's biography presents. After crises such as the loss of her two husbands, her thoughts invariably turned to the consolations of religion and spiritual meditation, and this constitutes a secondary theme or motif in this poem. The resignation that has finally come—"mi alma reposa al fin" ("my soul has found some peace at last")—is tempered by the belief that God wished for things to be this way ("Quísolo Dios y fue"): Te amé, no te amo ya: piénsolo al menos" ("I loved you but I do not love you now; at least I think that that is true"). Life has freed the lover from the loved one's spell, but the liberty thus gained is sad ("triste libertad") and Tula finds herself in a deep and vast solitude ("en honda y vasta soledad me miro"). The poem ends on a note of forgiveness ("generoso perdón") and affection ("cariño tierno").

There are other poems that we may likewise relate to the love affair with Cepeda. Several echo passages first found in love letters from Tula to her reluctant swain. One, "El porqué de la inconstancia" ("The Reason for Inconstancy"), (*OB* I, 282–283), is addressed to "mi amigo." Its theme of change-ableness in woman is obviously a reply to accusations of capriciousness and fickleness that la Avellaneda refutes. "Contra mi sexo te ensañas / y de inconstancia lo acusas" ("Against my sex you rage / and accuse us of inconstancy"), she begins, but she immediately turns the accusation back upon her lover, telling him to look into his own being and actions ("analizar en ti mismo / del alma humano el abismo"). In a letter dated April 15, 1840, written in Seville, the problem is explicit: "Tu me has dicho, juzgándome por ajenas opiniones, que soy inconstante" ("You have told me, judging from the opinions of others, that I am inconstant"), Tula writes. Some lines later, however, she points out that Cepeda himself was the fickle one: "Ultimamente he sabido positivamente que otras distracciones más nuevas te ocupaban en las horas en que yo suspiraba por verte . . ." ("Lately I have learned definitely that other and newer distractions took up your time while I was sighing to see you . . .").

After the first two stanzas, however, the poem takes on a philosophical tone sustained until the final lines. The theme of inconstancy is enlarged, tied to human weakness and the human condition, to all the "daughters of Eve" and "all the sons of Adam." The ultimate ideal is not something that we can attain because: "De amor y dicha tenemos / sólo un recuerdo nublado" ("Of love and happiness we have / only a clouded memory"). The joys of the past are "enterrado / bajo el árbol de edén!" ("buried / under the tree of Eden!"). The note of hopefulness of the last stanza relates this work to the first of the "A él" poems rather than the final one.

The "Soneto Imitando una oda de Safo" ("Sonnet Imitating an Ode of Sappho"), (*OB* I, 257–258), and the relatively lengthy "Amor y orgullo" ("Love and Pride") are also a part of the love poetry, the former less personal, as might be expected from a partial translation, and the second reflecting in its narrative the problems of love, pride, and self-esteem that are also a developed theme of the "love letters." The María of the narrative, like the author herself, is dark-haired, proud, and strong-willed, but love has humbled her. In part 2 of the poem, which

is Maria's song of love's torment, the image of the leaf in a
whirlwind again expresses the feelings of loss ("cual hoja seca
al raudo torbellino") and of powerlessness before destiny's bitter
strength ("cedo al poder del áspero destino"). The woman who
haughtily had disdained the suitors who had courted her, whose
capricious relationships ("lazos caprichosos") had been mere
pastime ("pasatiempo"), has been reduced to grief and bitterness ("duelo y amargura"). Here the portrait of the lover
suggests, as in the earlier "A él" poem, the figure of the satanic
avenger, one who had conquered and enslaved the arrogant
and cruel femme fatale whose cry of anguish is a kind of ex-
quisite pain ("de tu servidumbre haciendo alarde..."). In the
third and final division of the poem, reason and pride are again
defeated when the lover returns after days of separation. Love
has transformed the sadistic temptress into an innocent and
childlike victim.

Love can also paralyze the will and leave in its wake a spiritual
lassitude that la Avellaneda calls "tedium" and which was made
famous by Baudelaire as "spleen" and "ennui" in his *Flowers of
Evil*, a state of hypochondria and depression that often follows
exaltation, one of whose attributes is a sense of being morose
rather than the "choleric" usually associated with the word
today. It is the central theme of the sonnet "Mi mal" ("My
Torment"):

Mi mal

En vano ansiosa tu amistad procura
adivinar el mal que me atormenta;
en vano, amigo, conmovida intenta
revelarlo mi voz a tu ternura.

Puede explicarse el ansia, la locura
con que amor sus fuegos alimenta....
Puede el dolor, la saña más violenta,
exhalar por el labio su amargura....

Mas de decir mi malestar profundo,
no halla mi voz, mi pensamiento, medio,
y al indagar su origen me confundo:

pero es un mal terrible, sin remedio,
que hace odiosa la vida, odioso el mundo,
que seca el corazón.... ¡En fin, es tedio!

My Torment

To no avail, concerned, your friendship tries
to comprehend what causes my torment;
in vain, my friend, my voice in effort spent,
has sought to calm your tender sighs.

Passion's anguish we can recognize
or the madness flames of love foment....
We know that woe and pain most violent
Can find relief by venting bitter cries....

But I've not found the means, nor can impart,
what neither voice nor lips can yet express,
to name the source wherein my torments start.

There is no patent cure for this distress
that makes the world a limbo, dries the heart,
and stifles life. 'Tis tedium and weariness!

(*OB* I, 269–270)

We know from her letters that la Avellaneda was afflicted with this malady of paralysis of will at various periods of her life and that only by strength of character was she able to overcome the states of despondency and torpor that followed in the wake of love's disappointments.

One of these deep emotional shocks was the death of la Avellaneda's first husband, Pedro Sabater. As we saw in Chapter 1, the brilliant and successful young man who became her husband as the aftermath of a rupture with the omnipresent Cepeda died within three months of marriage. One poem, written to him, and in reply to a poem written by him to his future wife, is an acceptance of his suit. The tenderness and simple beauty of two of the final stanzas are particularly poignant in their truth. The "altar of the idol" of Cepeda has been destroyed, and so, recognizing the illness and the fragility of Sabater's health, she

offers him tenderness and willingness to share the future with
him:

> Yo no puedo sembrar de eternas flores
> La senda que corréis de frágil vida;
> Pero si en ella recogéis dolores,
> Un alma encontraréis que los divida.
> . . . .
> ¿Qué más podéis pedir? ¿Qué más pudiera
> Ofrecer con verdad mi pobre pecho?
> Ternura os doy con efusión sincera. . . .
> ¡De mi ídolo el altar ya está deshecho!

> Along the fragile path of life you tread,
> Undying blossoms I cannot thee provide,
> But if with pain its course is spread,
> Then in our souls your sorrows we'll divide.
> . . . .
> What more then can you ask? What more
> That this poor heart can give today?
> The tenderness and warmth I hold in store. . . .
> My idol's altar has been swept away!

(*OB* I, 301)

In addition to these *cuartetas* written during Sabater's court-
ship, Tula also dedicated two elegies to her first husband after
his death. The first bears the descriptive line, "Después de la
muerte de mi marido" ("After the Death of My Husband") and
begins with the heartrending lament "Otra vez llanto, soledad,
tinieblas..." ("Once more darkness, tears, and solitude..."),
(*OB* I, 304). Another illusion had gone up like smoke; the beloved light that shone briefly in her life disappeared as rapidly
as a bolt of lightning ("un relámpago fue"). Once more destiny
had sealed Tula's fate and destroyed her hopes. The poem ends
on a note of prayer for help "en este abismo de pavor profundo"
("in this abyss of profound dread") until the soul has left "del
mundo / la inmensa soledal" ("the immense solitude of the
world").

The second elegy, (*OB* I, 304–305), composed like the first,
while la Avellaneda was staying in the Convent of Lorette in

Bordeaux where Sabater had died, takes the form of a prayer. The theme of loneliness and deprivation is again developed, but the poetess conforms to God's will. She asks the nuns of the convent to care for the silent and cold sepulcher that she must leave on foreign soil.

III *The Theme of Poetry*

Critics agree that poetry was a passion of la Avellaneda's from early childhood on. She wrote from intuitive inspiration, however, and not from conscious theory. Although most of her poems follow the canons of romanticism, there are also works that we categorize as neoclassical in form, tone, and subject matter. We look in vain, nevertheless, for some kind of declaration of "school," for a manifesto or poem that might serve as an *ars poetica*. In nineteenth-century Spain—quite unlike France with the aesthetic pronouncements of a Hugo, a Gautier, a Verlaine, or a Rimbaud— only Gustavo Adolfo Bécquer, Tula's younger contemporary, has left us a consciously discernible body of work treating poetic theory. La Avellaneda writes poetry about poetry, but no formula emerges, no pronouncements on the how's and why's of the creating of poetry.

Such works as "A la poesía" ("To Poetry"), (*OB* I, 237–238), "El poeta" ("The Poet"), (*OB* I, 254–255), and separate poems written in homage or memory of poets she knew and admired, do give ample evidence of the exalted position which she accorded the poetic art. In the Spain of la Avellaneda's years of triumph—in contrast to the earlier years in England or France where such major figures of romanticism as Byron or Hugo were social heretics—the poet had become a respected figure. The elaborate ceremony for the "crowning" of Manuel José Quintana, together with various public manifestations of admiration for la Avellaneda herself, bear witness to this. Poets were honored at elaborate public occasions, attended and given approbation by the most prominent figures of social and political life, the royal family, ministers, the highest military personnages of the realm. By mid-century the youthful rebellion of Espronceda had given way to the complacent security of the man of letters whose death la Avellaneda duly laments in appropriate verses. Even

Heredia, the Cuban patriot dead in exile in Mexico, is glorified for his singing of the beauties of Niagara, not for his rebellious attitude in the face of Spanish repression in his homeland.

If the poet is a special figure, to be praised and publically honored, then poetry itself also must occupy an exalted rank. In "To Poetry," la Avellaneda's first words establish the position of poetry—"del alto cielo / precioso don" ("a precious gift from heaven") (*OB* I, 237),—with respect to the poet himself, an intimate relationship of "tú" ("thou"), a deeply participatory communication that both consoles ("de mis penas íntimo consuelo") and is a fountainhead of pleasure: ("De mis placeres manantial querido"). Even more: it is the soul of the world ("alma del orbe"), a vast and powerful creative force stemming from God himself ("¿Qué a tu dominio inmenso / no sujetó el Señor?"). Nature offers constant evidence of poetry's existence, in moon, sun, dawn, or evening, in the roaring hurricane at sea— an obvious reference to the great storm of Tula's first crossing of the Atlantic—or the sleepy murmur of the brook responding to the breeze's sigh, i.e., the small intimate voice that will be the soul and core of Bécquer's poetic expression, but sounds only a minor, albeit impressive, note in Tula's poems. The poet is privy to this world of beauty. Poetry dictates to the poet's lyre, and unfortunate is he who has no sense of poetry. The world for him is an empty temple ("templo vacío"). Tula herself, however, prays at Poetry's altar ("a tu ara santa") and asks only to sing in the shadow of those altars ("a la sombra feliz de tus altares").

IV Neoclassic Forms and Romantic Content

Although the poems discussed above place la Avellaneda within the mainstream of romanticism, there is in her poetry, as various critics have pointed out, a strong current of neoclassicism that is found particularly in the collection of 1841. Nature is present in these poems also, but it is that nature preferred by the neoclassicists, such as pastoral landscapes and peaceable scenes filled with flowers or with songbirds.

This idyllic vision predominates in the first stanzas of "La primavera" ("The Springtime"). Winter has gone, and the sun's bright shining has brought a benign warmth:

> Huyo el invierno sañudo
> y luce brillante el sol,
> que el pálido velo rasgando glorioso,
> difunde en la tierra benigno calor.

> The fierceness of winter I flee
> and brightly the sun does shine,
> for with glory rending the veiling so pale,
> it infuses the earth with warmth benign.

> (*OB* I, 262)

The once-frozen fields become covered with bright greenery ("Se cubre el campo aterido / can halagüeño verdor"). Spring's welcome smile, bestowing life. "Tu grata sonrisa, que vida difunde, / perfuma los aires y colora la flor" ("perfumes the air, colors the flowers"). The tone of tranquility and security characteristic of eighteenth-century optimism, however, is not sustained in the poem. Tula's temperament, the romantic *Weltschmerz*, sets the predominant tone of the final stanzas of the work, conveying its essential meaning. "Oh," she writes, "Why can you not also extend your favors to man?" ("¡Ay! ¿Por qué también al hombre / no se extiende tu favor?"). Man has only one fleeting springtime ("fugaz primavera"). Pain and disillusionment are his lot:

> Vuelves al árbol las flores,
> el perfume y el color....
> ¡Mas no das al hombre las flores perdidas!
> ¡Mas no le revives la muerta ilusión!

> To the tree you give back its flowers,
> Its perfume and its color....
> But man's vanished flowers you do not return!
> You do not revive the illusions that die!

> (*OB* I, 262)

This mixture of outward neoclassicism with the personal and intimate perplexities of the troubled romantic typifies a number of Tula's poems. One of the best known, "A mi jilguero" ("To My Goldfinch"), exemplifies this fusion of romantic plaint with neoclassical form. The poetess's pet goldfinch will not sing, despite the beauty of its cage and the care that is proffered it:

> En tu jaula preciosa
> ¿qué falta a tu recreo?
> Mi mano cariñosa
> previene tu deseo.

> In your cage so fine and grand,
> What lacks for pleasure's fare?
> My gentle and attentive hand
> Looks to your every care.

(*OB* I, 238)

Tula, however, comprehends her songbird's distress ("¡Mi corazón lo entiende!"), deploring its fate because when she weeps for the bird, she is also weeping for herself ("cuando tu pena lloro / ¡también lloro la mía!"). She then develops the central concept, portrayal of herself as the exile from the happy homeland of her childhood—the theme of the lost Eden of innocence and early youth. Unhappy like the goldfinch, Tula must forever live separated from her native soil, from her beloved Cuba:

> Que triste, cual tú, vivo
> por siempre separada
> de mi suelo nativo. . . .
> ¡de mi Cuba adorada!

> For sorrowful like you,
> from my own native soil
> separated I live . . .
> apart from the Cuba I love!

(*OB* I, 239)

The poetess then portrays the Cuba of her nostalgic memory,

the fertile fields, the Tinima River, the sounds and scenes of her childhood: "El sol de fuego, / la hermosa luna, / mi dulce cuna, / mi dulce hogar . . ." ("sun of fire, / the lovely moon, / my gentle cradle, / my gentle home . . .") (*OB* I, 239). Opening the cage, she gives the bird its freedom and her love ("¡libertad y amor te doy!"), and as recompense, asks only to hear the goldfinch's song of happiness as dawn begins to light her window.

A similarly pathetic note appears in most if not all of the early poems. In "A una mariposa" ("To a Butterfly"), (*OB* I, 243–244), the beauty of the butterfly is endangered by the thorns of the rosebush. In "El cazador" ("The Hunter"), (*OB* I, 244–245), the white dove shot by the hunter becomes a symbol for the young woman, Elvira, who has been seduced and abandoned. The hunter thereby emerges as a Don Juan figure who leaves death and destruction in his wake. In "A un niño dormido" ("To a Sleeping Child"), (*OB* I, 251), innocence has not yet been violated, but time will soon alter that, robbing the child of happiness ("que a robarte tal ventura / se apresta el tiempo tirano"). The winds of passion will becloud feelings ("del viento de las pasiones / será bien presto agitado"), and love, jealousy, and ambition will be the lot of the adult until finally, hope is gone and disillusionment takes its place ("se eclipsará la esperanza, / luciendo atroz desengaño").

V *Plentitude of Romanticism*

If Tula successfully incorporates her own innate romanticism into poems of a neoclassic bent, she nonetheless finds her fullest expression in those works where her temperament and emotions predominate. One series of poems, which form a romantic canon, treat a number of themes and subjects associated with the romantic movement in general, the moon ("A la luna"), the stars ("A las estrellas"), the sea ("Al mar"), destiny ("Al destino"), melancholy ("El genio de la melancolía"), cemeteries ("Cuartetos escritos en un cemeterio"), the glorification of freedom from civilization's restraints ("El beduino"), and various poems treating states of depression, insomnia, and emotional torment. In all cases, the poetess associates herself and her own psychic states either directly or through implication with the development of the poem.

"El beduino" ("The Bedouin") (*OB* I, 276), is a case in point. La Avellaneda's biography makes clear that she was rebellious as a child and as a young woman. Her strength of character and determination showed itself before the family left Cuba, and manifested itself again and again in personal matters such as her headstrong refusal to marry the suitors chosen for her. We may recall that her love affair with the poet Tassara resulted in the birth of an illegitimate daughter. The figure of the Bedouin, consequently, represents the author herself who exalts freedom from the restraints of the society in which she lived. Both the nomad and his horse are free to roam the vast desert for "que ni el freno tu boca maltrata / ni la ley mi feliz voluntad" ("neither the reins do harm to your mouth / nor law to my happy volition").

The Bedouin is also, of course, a variation of a stock type in romantic literature, that of the idealized outlaw, Byronic in his pose of strength and defiance, of which Espronceda's pirate is the best-known example in Spanish literature. We admire him as he urges on his swift steed to attack a caravan, defies the harsh environment in which he lives, and humbles all who enter into his domain. He knows the makings of civilization, power, wealth, talent, pride and science ("su poder, sus tesoros, / su talento, su orgullo, su ciencia"), but rejects it all. He and his are kings of vast deserts ("del desierto vastísimo reyes") where there are "sin las artes de frívolo ornato" ("no arts of frivolous adornment"), "y sin templos, palacios, ni leyes" ("nor temples, palaces, or laws").

In other poems, the personification of nature permits la Avellaneda to express her inner self, at times through contrast, as in the sonnet "Al sol" ("To the Sun") (*OB* I, 255), when the poetess asks the sun to bring warmth and light to her languid self. The sun of the land of her birth is invoked to dispel the mists of melancholy. "A la luna" ("To the Moon") (*OB* I, 266–267), embodies the contrast in the equation of past-happiness/present-sorrow. The moon has not changed, but the circumstances of the author have. The moon, witness to the happiness of the past—"Tú, que mis horas de placer miraste" ("You who watched my hours of pleasure")—is unperturbed in its course, casting its silver sheen across the sky ("argenta la extensión del cielo") and "sobre los campos y las gayas flores / perlas derraman" ("across the fields and bright flowers / scatters pearls"), but nothing can disperse the shadows on the poet's life.

"Al mar" ("To the Sea") (*OB* I, 242–243), epitomizes these tendencies. The use of fourteen-syllable alexandrines lends majesty to the theme, and the alternating rhyme of *verso llano* ("movimiento-pensamiento") with *verso agudo* ("bramar-reposar") suggests the rhythm of waves as well as the fluctuations of the poetess's spirit. The ocean is a colossus that represents for the romantic artist the primordial forces of life in its most savage potential, which la Avellaneda underscores in her opening stanzas. She endows the sea with inexplicable mystery: "Ni el vuelo de la mente tus límites alcanza" ("not even flights of imagination can conceive limits for you"), employing a series of nouns and adjectives that reinforce the sense of majestic awe and immensity that the ocean represents. The sea's movement is eternal ("tu eterno movimiento"), its roar horrifying ("el hórrido bramar"); the ocean becomes a vast solitude ("vasta soledad"); a domain of thunderous noises, of lightning and of mountainous waves. She asks if the spirit of this tumultuous sea is a blasphemous Lucifer ("segundo Lucifer").

The tumult of la Avellaneda's soul is greater, nevertheless, than that of the ocean:

> Si a veces nos alzamos terribles y violentas,
> vorágines abriendo con hórrido rugir,
> en tu alma se levantan más férvidas tormentas,
> que tu razón acaso no alcance a resistir.

> If on occasion waves rise up in fearful violence,
> Opening vast vortices with horrifying roar,
> There are within your soul far more awesome torments
> That your mind may be unable to endure.

> (*OB* I, 243)

But the sea also offers a spectacle of calm, as does life when time tempers both the joys and the anguish of the past. The golden dreams of youth ("sueños de oro, / del alba de la vida") will not return, yet the feverish activity of the poetess's life continues ("sigue de la vida la ardiente actividad"). In the final analysis, only the sure and inmutable rock of faith is a certainty, and the sea "¡Proclama la grandeza de tu divino Autor!" ("proclaims the greatness of its divine Author").

VI   *Meditations and Philosophical Speculation*

We have already seen in such a poem as "El porqué de la inconstancia" ("The Reason for Inconstancy") that la Avellaneda may treat an abstract concept such as fickleness in terms of her own personal and intimate experience. Thus, a philosophical theme or idea functions much as does nature in the poems discussed above. It is, consequently, arbitrary to set aside a portion of Tula's work as philosophical speculation as, for example, Raimundo Lazo has done.[3] It is his point, strongly made, that la Avellaneda's work was gravely affected by the romantic tendency to versify philosophical ideas and speculations. He tells us that the "temperament of the poetess did not lend itself to the play of poetic manipulation of abstractions," and that the two poems that Tula wrote on the subject of hope evince her inability to handle her theme while having to submit to the necessities of meter and rhyme schemes. He also indicates the pernicious effects of the bombastic and rhetorical aspects of romanticism in this category—if we can speak of it as such—on Tula's poetry. However, a poem such as "Al destino" ("To Destiny") (*OB* I, 287), bears a clear relationship to other poems and to the life experience of the poetess, making that work more than the mere exercise that Lazo's remarks would suggest. Destiny appears earlier in "The Departure" as "hado" or "fate," acquiring somber overtones ("Doquier que el hado en su furor me impela" ["Whatever in its fury fate now sends"]) which, in the light of subsequent events in the poetess's life, take on a sense of augury.

"To Destiny" was written after la Avellaneda's foreboding had been fulfilled in the form of her fatal love for Cepeda. The first ten lines of the poem, when related to this, take on an intensely personal tone as the poetess describes her unavailing efforts to free herself from the "fatal chain" and "harsh capitivity" ("la fatal candena"; "cautiverio rudo") to which heaven has condemned her. She can only return to the "yugo fatal" ("fatal yoke") despite the fact that the situation becomes ever more intolerable. The final lines, however, do sustain Lazo's criticisms. The rhetorical excesses, although obviously meant to convey the writer's anguish, give the effect of a poetic exercise. Such verses as "¡Héme equí! ¡Tuya soy! ¡dispón, destino, / de tu víctima dócil!" ("Here am I! I am yours! Dispose, destiny, / of your docile victim!") transform an otherwise moving plaint into melodrama that rings false.

If we accept the "Cuartetos escritos en un cemeterio" ("Quatrains Written in a Cemetery") (*OB* I, 269), as a meditation on death, la Avellaneda emerges as a skilled handler of this type of poetry of thematic development. While Tula utilizes the exclamation point and the imperative to disadvantage in this poem also, it is less obtrusive. The tone of gravity of the verse itself is particularly effective in expressing the stoic dignity with which the poetess elaborates her thought: "He aquí el asilo de la eterna calma, / do sólo el sauce desmayado crece" ("Here is the refuge of calmness eternal, / where only the willow tree languidly grows"). She calls to all those who from their cradle have gazed on the angry frown of destiny ("todos los que el ceno airado / del destino mirasteis en la cuna"). She ends the poem with a somber summary of her thought and feeling: "¡Que ilusión de la vida es la ventura, / mas la paz de la muerte es verdadera!" ("For happiness is life's illusion, / But the peace of death is no delusion!").

Another much lengthier poem, "El genio de la melancolía" ("The Spirit of Melancholy"), *OB* I, 297–298, likewise develops a meditative or philosophical theme. Noteworthy for more than its intrinsic beauty, it clearly anticipates in form and in imagery the far more famous *Riva V* of Bécquer. The latter develops two parallel concepts, one inspiration, and the other reason or conscious thought. His "tag line" tells us that only genius can bring the two together. The poem, consequently, forms part of the body of Bécquer's work that concerns itself with poetic and creative theory. Something of this is anticipated in la Avellaneda's final lines, the notion that melancholy was born from ardent hope and sad memory, i.e., passion recollected in tranquillity and thereby modified by the conscious mind ("Nací de la ardiente esperanza / y el triste recuerdo").

More striking, however, is the subtle and vague imagery of
the poem that clearly foreshadows the ephemeral atmosphere
of vaporous mists, whispering sounds, and diaphonous nature
fundamental to the poetic world of Bécquer. As in Bécquer's
Rima also, the spirit of melancholy speaks. The reiterated "Yo
soy" ("I am") in the poems of both Tula and Bécquer renders
comparison inevitable. The poem begins as follows:

> Yo soy quien ·abriendo las puertas del ocaso,
> al sol le prepara su lecho en cristales,
> yo soy quien recoge sus luces postreras,
> que acarician las tibias esferas.

> I am he who opening the gates of eventide
> a couch of crystal for the sun provide,
> I am he who gathers up the waning light,
> that caresses the tepid spheres of night.

> (*OB* I, 297)

The minor tone and delicate atmosphere established by the half
light of eventide or of reflected light is developed further by
such imagery as "pálida tarde" ("pale afternoon"), color including purple and "purpura y nacar" ("mother-of-pearl"), and gentle
natural effects embodied in breezes, the murmur of the water
of a river, the spume raised on it, the rays of the moon:

> Yo soy quien murmura del río en las aguas,
> rizando sus ondas de cándida espuma;
> yo soy quien se mece con blando desmayo
> de la luna en el nítido rayo.

> I am he who murmurs in the river's waters,
> curling up its waves with gleaming foam;
> I am he who cradled in a bland tender swoon
> am rocked in the luminous ray of the moon.

VII   *Religious Poetry*

In the edition of her lyric poetry of 1841, la Avellaneda included only one religious poem. By the edition of 1850, there

were twelve. This reinforces what we know of the continuously deepening spiritual crises of the author in those years, and of her increasing dependence on religion as solace for her anguish and pain. We must remember, however, that Christianity in the romantic period has certain characteristics that would not, for example, be found in an eighteenth-century poet. The rationalistic approach had been replaced by emotion. Chateaubriand in France, and through his writings much of Western Europe, had laid the foundations for a new religious sensitivity. Religion spoke to the heart and soul, not to the intellect. God was manifest everywhere that there was beauty, in the sunlight streaming through the stained glass windows of a cathedral, in the reflection of mountains in the blue still waters of a lake, or in the power and majesty of a great storm. The receptive soul could feel God through His manifestations around us, and through a simple and accepting faith. It is in these terms that we must see la Avellaneda's religious poetry, and not, as some critics would have it, as a failure to comprehend profound or telling theological concepts. Although in her own day she was compared favorably with Saint John of the Cross, we can no longer see her devotional works in the same light.

There are several thematic developments which la Avellaneda follows in her religious poems, including several to the Virgin Mary, to Christ, some on the theme of the Redemption, and still others that meditate on God, Eternity, and the Deity's ways toward man. These poems are predictably grave in tone as befits their subject matter, but a difference of attitude separates those works of a less personal nature—those that imitate or suggest biblical themes and inspiration—from those later poems in which notes of personal anguish and of mystical longing predominate. God as the inspirer of poetry constitutes another important theme. In "Dedicacion de mi lira a Dios" ("Dedication of My Lyre to God"), (*OB* I, 356-358), the poetess, as in "To Poetry," envisions God as the source of poetry and beauty in nature, of harmony, and of genius. Man, by contrast, appears as a humble and ephemeral being, a shadow that passes, an anxious hope ("sombra que pasa"; "inquieta esperanza").

The poems to the Virgin take something of the same form. What begins as a hymn of praise becomes a vehicle for the ex-

pression of the poetess's personal afflictions, as in the work "A
la Virgen, Plegaria" ("To the Virgin, Supplication"). (*OB* I, 262–
263). Written in 1841, at the time of the author's disappointment
over Cepeda, the poem employs the central image of a ship that
flounders without compass or pilot near the reefs ("Mi bajel
navega incierto...."). The Virgin, in that dark night, is pure
light, the beacon that helps the weak and brings happiness to
those who are sad:

> Vos en la noche sombría
> Pura luz, celeste faro,
> De los débiles amparo,
> De los tristes alegría...
>
> You in the dark of the night,
> Celestial lantern, purest of light,
> For those that are weak, firm support,
> For those that are sad, new delight...

> (*OB* I, 262)

It is to her that la Avellaneda turns for help in her torment and
pain: "Ved mi vida abandonada / ¡Madre amada:" There follows
a perhaps exaggerated catalog of reasons for the anguish of
the poetess, her youth without love ("Mi juventud sin amores"),
her joyless childhood ("mi infancia no tuvo risas") and her
fears that she will have no one in her old age ("Ni mi vejez
tendrá apoyo"). She characterizes herself as an orphan at an
early age ("¡La orfandad meció mi cuna!") as well as an exile
both from her native land ("no existe / ni patria ni hogar
querido"), and in life in general as she is an "extranjera en este
mundo" ("alien in this world"), (*OB* I, 262).

However, in such relatively lengthy poems as "La cruz" ("The
Cross"), (*OB* I, 310–312), and "Dios y el hombre" ("God and
Man"), (*OB* I, 270–273), the personal note is avoided. The former
offers a lyrical summation of the significance of the cross as
symbol for all of humanity. The recurring phrase "¡Alzad la
cruz!" ("Lift up the cross") sets the tone of high praise main-
tained through the work. The latter poem, "God and Man," was
written after a reading of the Book of Job, and, as in that book

of the Bible, man's inability and inadequacy in the understanding of God and His ways is stressed. Man asks what is the essence of Deity ("¿Quién eres? dice a Dios, ¿Cuál es tu esencia?"), but his intelligence and his studies of nature and the world cannot comprehend God. God replies to man that His powers and His plans are beyond the comprehension of either wise men or astronomers ("Tus sabios, tus astrónomos profundos, / podrán decir cómo hago inalterable / la eterna ley") (*OB* I, 270). And man, who cannot understand the great mysteries of nature, cannot fathom even the depths of his own being ("¿Y no eres un abismo / ¡oh, átomo pensador! para ti mismo?"), (*OB* I, 272). God has engraved the idea of His being in man's soul as He has in Nature; man can only stand in silent awe ("el humano saber calle y se asombre"). (*OB* I, 273).

VIII *Other Thematic Tendencies*

In addition to the thematic tendencies studied above, there are several other categories into which Gertrudis's poems may be divided. One, which grew with the years and Tula's ever-increasing fame, is that of poems written for special occasions. These are primarily of topical interest to us today, and may be read with interest by the literary historian, but their intrinsic merit as poetry seems scant by present standards. Several such poems were written on the death of famous poets. These include "A la muerte de don José María de Heredia" ("On the Death of don José María de Heredia"), (*OB* I, 255–257), "A la muerte del joven y distinguido poeta don José de Espronceda" ("On the Death of the Youthful and Distinguished Poet don José de Espronceda"), (*OB* I, 274–275), and "En la muerte del laureado poeta Señor don Manuel José Quintana" ("On the Death of the Poet Laureate don Manuel José Quintana"), (*OB* I, 331). Tula had written, in addition, a special poem for Quintana's coronation as poet laureate which she read at the ceremony. There are also poems on the coming-of-age of Isabella II, for the queen's birthday, and for special occasions in the lives of family and friends. In Cuba, various poems of the same type were written, one being on the occasion of the dedication of a statue of Christopher Columbus in the city of Cárdenas.

Besides the poems on the theme of Cuba, there are several on themes of Spain, notably the "Paseo por el Betis' '("Going Along the Betis"), (*OB* I, 247–248), which describes a boatride along the Guadalquiver at Seville (the ancient name for the Guadelquiver River was the Betis), and "Al árbol de Guernica" ("To the Tree of Guernica"), (*OB* I, 336–337). The latter is a poem praising the famous oak tree af the Basques that symbolizes for the Basque people their ancient liberties, just as Guernica has become, through its destruction in the Spanish Civil War and the masterwork of Picasso commemorating the event, a symbol of resistance to tyranny. Another poem, "El pescador" ("The Fisherman"), (*OB* I, 330), is set in San Sebastián, although the geographical references are such that any seascape would be equally fitting.

No discussion of la Avellaneda's lyrical accomplishments would be complete without some mention of her translations. Tula herself uses the word "imitación" ("imitation") to describe these. She does not pretend to give the reader a literal rendering in Spanish of the original, but rather, a reworking in the second language. Two sonnets are based on works of Sappho and of Petrarch; another "imitates" a portion of the *Childe Harold* of Byron. The remainder are taken from the French, and are much more numerous. Several are from the major French romantic poets Victor Hugo and Alphonse de Lamartine. Others are based on works of the lesser-known Evariste Désiré de Parny, a poet born on the island colony of Reunion and belonging primarily to the period of neoclassicism (1753–1814).

IX *Technical Virtuosity*

La Avellaneda is justly renowned for her technical virtuosity, employing an impressive variety of forms, meters, and rhyme schemes. These include long-established forms such as the *romance*, of eight syllables, the *romancillo* of hexameters, the *endecha* (which is a kind of dirge), the *redondilla* with a rhyme scheme of abba, the *quintilla* five-lined stanza, the *octavilla aguda* eight-lined stanza, and the *octava*, both the standard "real" (*a b a b a b c c*) and the "Italiana" (*a a b c c b d d*). In cultivating the sonnet form, Tula is unique in the romantic period, having composed a dozen including "On Leaving" and "My Lament."

In addition to these forms, la Avellaneda experimented with new or infrequently utilized meters and rhyme schemes, or employed traditional lines in innovative combinations. She thereby ranks with her contemporary Espronceda, and like him in his "El estudiante de Salamanca" ("Student of Salamanca"), ranges from bisyllabic verse to lines of sixteen syllables. The poem "Noche de insomnio y alba" ("Night of Insomnia and Dawn"), (*OB* I, 287–288), interesting for itself, is a veritable tour de force. In it, Gertrudis moves from the opening lines of two syllables to verses of three, five, eight, ten, twelve, fourteen, and finally sixteen syllables. The traditional Spanish verse lines of eight and eleven syllables predominate in Tula's poetry as a whole, however.

While la Avellaneda shows herself a master of form, she is less distinguished in her imagery or in her use of vocabulary or qualifying adjectives. Raimundo Lazo severely criticizes her in this area,[4] listing the clichés and the limp adjectivation such as "verdes hojas," "bello jardín," "negro manto de la noche" ("green leaves," "lovely garden," "black cloak of night"), and so on. Her imagery is simply that of her times, and as we have seen, partakes of both neoclassicism and of romanticism. We find with frequency, for example, poetry metaphorically represented as lyre or harp, while the cypress stands for melancholy and death, and such flowers as the rose and the violet, for brief moments of beauty and happiness.

Consequently, la Avellaneda's fame as a poetess rests less on innovation in the area of poetic usage than in her enormous talent for expression within the modes of her time and the skill with which she interwove even those materials that were becoming hackneyed by usage in the hands of poets of lesser stature.

CHAPTER 3

The Dramatic Works

U NTIL the twentieth century, the theater was almost exclusively a man's world. By the nineteenth century, woman had, of course, become firmly established as actresses and were celebrated for their successes on the stage even though they were looked down upon socially because of their profession. A woman playwright was another matter. Although some women did make significant contributions to the literature of drama before the present century, we have to search hard to find even a brief mention of them. In France in the 1840s and early 1850s, Madame de Girardin, née Delphine Gay, had several successful productions in Paris. George Sand, so prolific in the novel, did write some twenty plays, but never achieved the success as dramatist that she did as novelist. In Spain, two women writers of the Golden Age, known for their poetry, also tried their hand at drama— María de Zayas y Sotomayor and Mariana Carvajal y Saavedra— but their dramatic works have not survived.[1] Only in England do we find any female figures in the annals of theater whose achievements are comparable to those of la Avellaneda. In the seventeenth century, Aphra Behn, who also wrote poetry and novels, reputedly had five plays on the boards in London at the same time. In the early eighteenth century, Susanna Centlivre, saw works produced that were to be staged in later generations up to 1900.[2]

La Avellaneda's career in Spain as a dramatist is, consequently, all the more impressive. She has left us a body of plays that compare favorably with those of any of the better-known male playwrights of her time, whether the duke of Rivas, García Gutiérrez, Hartzenbush, or Zorrilla. While Tula's reputation has subsisted through her lyrical poetry, it might well be argued that

78

her renown should rest instead on her dramatic creativity. Even the first play of hers to be produced, *Leoncia*, is all of a piece, a more finished work in some ways than her first novel, *Sab*, which was written during the same period of her life.

As we know, Gertrudis began writing plays as a child in Puerto Príncipe, directing and acting in them herself. None of these has come down to us, but the genre was not new to her when she decided to do something professional. The extent of what she accomplished in the field can be best measured when we realize that she wrote sixteen full-length dramas, twelve of them in verse, and three short plays, plus one full-length translation from the French. In 1852, five of her plays—four of them successes—opened in Madrid; in 1855, three opened.[3] Several of her works, the trage- dies *Munio Alfonso*, *Saúl*, and *Baltasar*, and the comedy *La hija de las flores*, were not only successes, but hailed as veritable tri- umphs and masterpieces of the art of drama. Newspaper reports of the openings recount the brilliant society that attended, includ- ing the royal family, leading figures of the period, and the top critics, and describe the ovations and laurel crownings of the author for one production after another.

All were not moments of glory, however. There were unpleas- ant episodes as well, the most serious being the one which, as we have described, took place at the opening of *Los tres amores*. Even before that, the jealousies and antipathy which Tula's suc- cesses engendered had deeply embittered her. To what extent the antagonisms were intensified by the fact that la Avellaneda was a woman who had invaded a career field that was considered exclusively male cannot be clearly determined. It was undoubtedly an important factor in provoking the unpleasantness in which envy and malice had a decided role.

Tula's aesthetic formation in the drama, as in the case of her lyric poetry, was highly eclectic. Her youthful readings, as noted earlier, included the French classical playwrights Corneille and Racine, and by the age of twelve or thirteen, the child prodigy had written a tragedy entitled *Hernán Cortes* about which she talked years later with her Madrid friend and mentor, Nicomedes Pastor Díaz. Consequently, as with her poetry, her drama cannot be easily categorized. She could write a tragedy such as *Munio Alfonso* coinciding with the dramatic conventions of Spanish romanticism—set in the Middle Ages and telling a tale of passion and violence—but she also transcends these tendencies. Her great biblical dramas resuscitated a type of play that had disappeared from the Madrid stage years before: the classical tragedy that reached its heights in France a century earlier. Tula did not observe the unities, but molded the form to fit her own concepts. Her comedies were also successfully staged and make good reading still today.

Conflict is, of course, the very stuff of drama. Without it in some form or other, no play can hold an audience, even now. In the romantic period, the tension and stress of conflict was highly pronounced, whether between individuals with resultant physical violence and bloodshed or between an individual and the society whose norms and exigencies were forced upon him. La Avellaneda was fully romantic in this sense. The conflict between the norms of society and her own passions and instincts lasted throughout her life. Consequently, it is not surprising that these same conflicts find expression in the plays in various forms and under differing guises. As with the poetry, her drama is fundamentally autobiographical, some of it in overtly identifiable passages or situations and elsewhere (as in the tragedies) covertly, but nevertheless recognizably related to situations or feelings in the author's life. The frustrations of the love affair with Cepeda, and even passages from the love letters to him, are transposed in the comedies, with the frustrations and emotional tortures of real life worked out in a happy ending. In the tragedies, however, love brings death and madness in its wake. The seeming glories and victories of the public figures are hollow when, at the very height of their triumphs, they must struggle with private pain, suffering, and frustration. Destiny does not free us from its coils. The individual is surrounded by uncontrollable forces. The soaring of the heart, the expansion of the ego, the surge of creative impulse, all run afoul of the rock of society's restrictions, incomprehension, and the bitter exigencies of reality.

Several things are characteristic of the dramatic production of la Avellaneda. The virtuosity for which she has remained justly celebrated in her lyrical poetry, and her phenomenal ability in handling a variety of verse structures, carries over to the dramas in verse form. Even those plays that were not successful stage productions were consistently praised for their versification. There are further links with the lyrical poetry in numerous passages of delicate and poignant beauty which, although they are not anthologized, could be as easily read out of their context as any of her other poems. In this sense, Tula's plays recall the lyric moments of Lope de Vega with their celebration of moments of plentitude and happiness. Her plots are equally intricate, overly so for our times and more appropriate for the operatic stage today, but nevertheless impressively handled and skillfully manipulated.

Thematically also, the plays relate to the poems. Many themes reappear, sometimes in similar form, in the dramas. Love is fundamental, and is developed in various guises. In its romantic form, it is the all-enveloping, volcanic emotion that becomes obsessive and borders on madness or brings insanity in its wake. Frequently presented as thwarted love, it is the central point of conflict that motivates the action. Sinful love in conflict with innocent love is another of the underlying themes that la Avellaneda returns to in different forms. The seducer figure, a satanic male who despoils his innocent victim of her purity and peace of heart, reappears. Bitterness, loneliness, and despair mark the heroines. When the men in the plays are virtuous, they are either the figure of the father or they in their turn are spurned and suffer in a kind of reversal of roles. Religion as solace, the beauty of nature, filial duty and family attachments, jealousy, egotism, hubris, and above all, the problems surrounding forced marriages are woven into the fabric of play after play. Death, as might be expected in romantic drama, is found in violent and bloody form in the tragedies, but it appears in lighter guise in the straight plays as well.

All of Tula's dramas depend on plot rather than character development for their essential interest. In this sense, they are the descendants of the drama of the great Golden Age playwrights of Spain. We can look in vain for a Hamlet or a Lear, but then there is no character of that stature anywhere in Occidental drama in the nineteenth century. Even though Zorilla's *Don Juan Tenorio* has survived on the boards each All Saint's Day in Hispanic countries, the protagonist is hardly an example of profound characterization. The despairs and confrontations of the figures in romantic drama may well seem larger than life, but we must remember that neither in it nor in the postromantic theater to which la Avellaneda's works in some ways belong, was there realistic theater. No real pretentions were made to the "slice-of-life" realism that was to develop later in the century.

Tula masterfully handles complications and sudden turns of plot, relying heavily on the proverbial triangle, i.e., two men in love with the same woman, or two women vying for the same man. Frequently the denouements are almost tantamount to the endings, which are so short that the curtain is ready to fall when the plot complications are finally unraveled, whether in drama, comedy, or tragedy. Conversely, lyrical passages or the use of spectacle and of music alleviate the story and change pace and texture. One of the impressive things about Tula's dramatic talent is that it seems to have sprung forth full-grown like Venus from the forehead of Zeus. The first professional play that she attempted, *Leoncia*, is a finished piece of playwriting, and contains in some form or other much of what would be utilized in her subsequent works, as we have outlined above.

I Leoncia

At the time of the drafting of *Leoncia*, in 1839 and 1840, la Avellaneda was residing in Seville. Her love affair with Cepeda was uppermost in her mind, but the first break had already taken place. Tula had not yet decided to leave Seville for Madrid, and as we know from her letters to Cepeda, she desperately hoped that her lover would come to the opening of this play which, we can well surmise, was written to communicate her tempestuous passion. She was a woman spurned, a woman determined, and a woman in severe torment. It is the heroine Leoncia through whom she expresses her feelings.

The mainspring of the action is a love triangle. The Oedipal overtones are omnipresent. Don Carlos is a young man, just twenty-six, in love with a woman in her thirties, Leoncia. There is something mysterious about Leoncia. Carlos's gossipy friend, don Gaspar de Rivera, tells the youth that the woman he loves has a wealthy older lover, and that all Madrid knows about this. Carlos had been interested, even in love with a girl now fifteen, Elena, who is of good family, obviously a proper match for him, and who is also in love with him. Carlos's father, don Fernando, decides to arrange a marriage with Elena, who has something mysterious in her past. She is the adopted rather than the blood daughter of don Luis de Castro. This fact is mentioned, but not stressed, as is the mysterious background of the supposed femme fatale that Leoncia represents.

Don Fernando's decision to arrange the marriage between Carlos and Elena, the first plot complication, is quickly followed by another: Carlos goes to see Leoncia, who is distressed that she has not seen him in over a day. She tells him: "Cuánto he padecido con tu tardanza! Sólo existo cuando estoy junto a ti . . ." ("How I have suffered by your latecoming! I only exist when I am by your side . . ."). It is their destiny to love: "nuestro destino es amarnos, siempre amarnos!" ("our destiny is to love each other, always to love each other!"). Carlos affirms his love and his impatience with "esta guerra interior que me despedaza" ("this war inside of me that tears me to pieces").[4] The count (el Conde de Peñafiel) who is supposedly her lover comes to the house, and when Leoncia insists on going to see him, Carlos, in a jealous rage, leaves, thinking himself betrayed by the woman whose hand he has so ardently sought.

Interestingly, the potential for dramatic exaggeration of the figure of Leoncia as an enigma is one that Tula handles with skill and equanimity. The result is an unusual but still believable woman. She has been described as a colossal figure and compared with Phedra and Jocasta,[5] but she does not struggle sufficiently with her ultimate problem to reach the stature of either classical character. Had Tula worked with the same material later in a less impassioned period of her life, she might have succeeded, but the emotions were too immediate for lengthy or impassive reflection. Leoncia's rival, Elena, epitomizes innocent beauty, as yet untouched and unstained by life's vicissitudes, the embodiment of that innocence which was taken from Leoncia when she was young by a treacherous and contemptible seducer.

In the third act, Leoncia learns of the projected marriage plans when she and Carlos are at a ball. They meet on a terrace and Leoncia declares that she cannot live without Carlos' love: "Ahora, tú decidirás mi destino. He luchado en vano largo tiempo contra una pasión que ya es omnipotente. Esas horas en que el temor horroroso de perderte destrozaba mi corazon, me han probado que ya no puedo vivir sin tu amor" ("Now you will decide my destiny. I have struggled in vain for a long time against a passion that is omnipotent. These hours in which the horrifying fear of losing you tore my heart apart have proven to me that I cannot live without your love"), (*OB* III, 660).

The verbal encounter of the two lovers rings too true to be without some foundation in the real-life scenes between Gertrudis and the reticent Cepeda. The letters reflect these encounters, one of which took place at a theater performance in Seville, but here in *Leoncia* they are given full form and substance, far stronger in tone than in the poems where we may clearly perceive their outlines. Line after line proclaims Leoncia's—and Tula's—anguish at her abandonment and betrayal: "He venido al encuentro de mi destino, en busca de mi sentencia, y ella ha sonado en mis oídos por otra voz que no era la tuya.... Por una voz terrible... siniestra... que salía del Infierno, sin duda... cuyos primeros sonidos han hecho temblar mi corazón con su presentimiento horroroso!" ("I have come to a meeting with my destiny, in search of my sentence, and it has sounded in my ears with a voice that was not yours.... With a terrible voice... sinister... which came from the Inferno no doubt...,whose first sounds made my heart tremble with a horrible presentiment!"); "¡Destino de maldición! ¡Ya se ha cumplido!" ("Destiny of damnation! Now it has been fulfilled!"); "¡Engañada siempre, abandonada..., víctima de la fatalidad y la perfidia! ¡Cuando he dado mi corazón, sólo le han admitido para hacerle pedazos, y luego me lo han arrojado con desprecio, sangriento y despedazado!" ("Always deceived, abandoned..., victim of fate and of perfidy! When I have given my heart, it has been accepted only to be torn into pieces, and thrown aside with contempt, bloody and cut to bits"), (*OB* III, 666).

In act 4, Leoncia is ill with a nervous crisis of a type that la Avellaneda herself suffered throughout her life, and which she mentions in various letters still extant. The count comes to console her. He is not, of course, Leoncia's lover, but a kind and thoughtful friend, a father or "uncle" figure. Leoncia, consequently, has been unjustly maligned, just as the Tula of real life was gossiped about. The count, however, does know the mystery of Leoncia's past. She had been seduced as a young girl, and had had an illegitimate daughter who perished in a storm at sea with Leoncia's mother. Leoncia set out from Venice, where she had lived with her parents, to find her seducer. Rich but unhappy, she finally settled in Madrid. The illegitimate child of the play and the abandonment of which Leoncia speaks, in the light of later events of Tula's life, take on the tones of premonition. Gertrudis' own daughter and her abandonment by the poet Tassara, as seen in the biographical chapter, constituted a deeply distressing time for la Avellaneda.

Leoncia, in a frenzy bordering on madness, goes to the house of Elena in disguise an hour before the marriage of Carlos and Elena is to take place. The bride has had two bad omens. In the garden a blackbird turned three times over her head and would not leave her. Later on, as she was dressing, she dropped and broke a bracelet in which she carried a picture of her grandmother. When Leoncia arrives, Carlos follows her and declares his love for her, but Leoncia is in a state of delirium. She hears the voice of Elena singing a song that her own mother had sung, with a voice that she thinks is her mother's. Then she sees the broken picture and realizes that it is Clothilde, her own mother. Then comes the typical recognition scene: grandmother and granddaughter had survived the shipwreck; Don Luis had married Leoncia's mother and adopted Elena as his daughter and heir; and Elena is Leoncia's long-lost daughter. Leoncia's love as a mother transforms her. Insisting that Carlos swear to give Elena every happiness, she resolves to go into a convent. At this point, however, the authoress springs her final surprise.

Elena's father leaves the room to bring back Carlos' father, don Fernando, whom Leoncia has never met. When she sees him, she recognizes the seducer of her youth and the natural father of Elena. The young couple, Carlos and Elena, who almost were married, are actually half-brother and sister. Leoncia draws a dagger and rushes toward don Fernando, but Elena turns the dagger on herself and falls dead as she curses the man who has made her life an inferno.

The hysteria of Leoncia and the crescendo of plot unraveling and of violence at the very end of the play are identifiably the material of romantic drama and of melodrama. La Avellaneda herself felt that this early work was without merit[6] and did not include it in her *Obras completas*. Nevertheless, it is an interesting work and does foreshadow later works and shed light on attitudes found elsewhere in the poetry and prose of the author. The play was enough of a success in the provincial theaters in which it played in 1840 to merit comment in a Madrid newspaper,[7] and it gave Tula sufficient confidence to begin a career of playwriting. In addition to the excesses of the ending, the play contains an overabundance of dramatic situations that involve illegitimacy, insanity, jealousy, the theme of unhappy marriage and of forced marriages, incest, mistaken or masked identity, alienation or social withdrawal, gossip, fatalism, religion as potential refuge, friendship, and love. Leoncia's wounded vanity and the all-powerful passions of the human heart are the obvious explanations for her near-madness and her hysterical behavior. Her betrayal in her innocent youth, her remorse, and finally her nobility and sense of sacrifice when faced with the reality of her own daughter's future are the means of her redemption.

Had the theme of incest not muddied the final moments of the work, it might have better stood the test of time. Although the play ends tragically, Tula was careful not to label the work a tragedy. There are several reasons for this. The setting is contemporary and much of the work, dialogue, daily relationships, social life, and milieu, are more the stuff of the bourgeois tragedy and comedy of the later nineteenth century than the high tradition of tragedy which la Avellaneda herself follows. Whether this could have been a comedy—in the sense of non-tragic, and not in the sense of comic—of manners if the impressionable Tula had not been reading the story of the excitable *Corinne* of Madame de Staël makes interesting speculation.[8] Nevertheless, Gertrudis' observations of behavior and of conduct do ring true. The romantic excesses borrowed from the literature of the period would seem to subvert her natural talents in the writing of the dramas, as happened so often in her poetry.

II Munio Alfonso

La Avellaneda's second play to be produced, *Munio Alfonso*, was a resounding success in Madrid where it opened on June 13, 1844. In the years between *Leoncia* and *Munio Alfonso,* the author had moved to Madrid and earned a reputation as a major poet. Her first volume of poetry and her first novel had been published. The production of this new play established her as a major figure in the world of the Madrid theater and brought her both triumphs and conflict.

Gertrudis entitled the work a tragedy. The dramatic situation on which the plot depends involves, as in *Leoncia,* the frustrations and complications arising from the social and political obligations which affect the development of the love of the two major characters, the Prince don Sancho of Castille and Munio Alfonso's daughter Fronilde. Neither don Sancho nor Fronilde have freedom of choice. The prince is betrothed to doña Blanca, infanta of the Kingdom of Navarre, in the hopes that such a union will prevent further fratricidal wars between two Christian kingdoms. As the action progresses, Munio Alfonso promises his daughter's hand to Count don Pedro. In the one case, reasons of state, and in the other, filial duty, preclude a happy issue of the love affair. Fronilde and Sancho are the most obvious individuals caught in the web of social demands and norms, but as the play progresses, we find that no one fully escapes. Doña Blanca does not love don Sancho nor does she want to marry him. When she inadvertently learns of the true feelings between her betrothed and Fronilde, she is relieved that their union will not take place: "Desgracia fuera interminable, horrible, / si nuestra triste unión la consumara..." ("An interminable misfortune, a horrible one it might have been / had our unhappy union consummated it...") (*OB* II, 38). Sancho tells doña Blanca: "Cual vos, señora, destinado a un yugo / que no eligió mi corazón, sellaba / el respeto filial los labios míos" ("As in your case, señora, destined for a yoke / that my heart did not elect, my lips / were sealed by filial respect"), (*OB* II, 38). In the final analysis, it is Munio himself who suffers most from a social conditioning that destroys his private person and his life.

There has been considerable critical discussion concerning the major thrust and focus of the drama, whether on the starcrossed lovers, or on Munio Alfonso. The question has centered primarily on act 4. Contemporary critics as well as later students of the play have argued that once Munio has killed his daughter, the dramatic action of the work ceases to have meaning, that the only point of the final act is "to give Munio the chance for Christian expiation of his crime."[9] There is no doubt that the love between don Sancho and Fronilde is central to the action of the play, and that it maintains interest as a boldly tragic story. The work could have been sustained with a short denouement after the father has murdered his innocent daughter, but in that case would hardly have been named *Munio Alfonso*, with all that the title implies for the interpretation of the purpose of the author. La Avellaneda even changed the title from *Alfonso Munio* to *Munio Alfonso*, implying that the story is meant to be primarily his, and not that of his daughter and her lover.

Both Fronilde and Sancho are youthful figures of the mold of Romeo and Juliet or the lovers of Teruel. It has been suggested that la Avellaneda was trying to emulate the test of character of Corneille's *Cid*,[10] but there is nothing between the two lovers here of the high and tortured moral drama that preoccupies don Rodrigue and Chimène. They do not rationalize their struggle to find a way out of their dilemma. Doña Blanca's decision not to accept the hand of the prince, and the benevolent collaboration of don Sancho's mother, the Empress doña Berenguela, bring about a relatively easy solution. This is the tragic irony of the situation. The problems of dynasty and state have been circumvented. We might say that at the very moment of the tragic act of homicide, love has conquered all. The Oedipal blindness of the father to his daughter's innocence and to the honorable intention of the man he believes seduced Fronilde precipitates the tragedy of the lovers. It is with the tragedy of the father that the fourth act is concerned.

Even though Gertrudis changed the denomination of the play from its original *tragedia* to *drama trágico*, it is obvious that she is fully aware of the neoclassical concepts and rules governing the writing of tragedy. She does not follow the unities, but she has not lost the fundamental Aristotelian precept of the eminent hero brought low by fate and flaw. Munio, at the peak of his glory when he returns after his great victory over the Moors, is honored and his praises sung by high and low alike.

His hubris does not lie in his heroic stature, however, but in his feelings for his daughter. When the archbishop tells him of his fears that don Sancho is subject to the wiles of one of the young women of the court, Munio speaks out in indignation, denouncing the unknown woman in the strongest terms, and in the bitter irony of his ignorance, highly praises the virtue of his own daughter. Fronilde, as we know, is virtuous and guiltless, and so there is a compounding of the tragic irony of the play. Munio's finest purposes are destroyed by his own rash act of filicide, bringing death, tragedy, and destruction to all about him. His penance is to fight the Moors in defense of religion and monarchy.

The story of Munio Alfonso is one that la Avellaneda took from chronicles of dubious historical accuracy. She believed Munio to be a direct ancestor of her father, and for that reason dedicated the 1869 version of the play to her brother Manuel as a direct descendant of Munio. However, it has been pretty well established that Munio Alfonso was not a historical character. There is no listing of him among the *alcaldes* of Toledo or the nobles at the time when supposedly he lived.[11] Whether he was fact or fable is aesthetically of less importance than Tula's belief that Munio was a historical figure, and her presentation of his and Fronilde's story in a play that was a triumphal success for her in every way. *Munio Alfonso* is a worthy successor to the great dramas of honor of the Spanish Golden Age works of Lope de Vega or of Calderón de la Barca, and the first of several historical plays that were to continue this same tradition in the later productions of la Avellaneda.

III El príncipe de Viana

El príncipe de Viana (*The Prince of Viana*), a second historical play, opened at the Teatro de la Cruz in Madrid on October 7, 1844. Although critical acclaim was less fervent than for *Munio Alfonso,* the production was another success. Some of the adverse reviews affected Tula deeply, and may be considered the first of the unmerited and scurrilous attacks that were to disturb her throughout much of the rest of her life.

The play is written in three acts and in verse, and is also subtitled *drama trágico*. Gertrudis took the subject matter from Manuel José Quintana's *Vidas de españoles célebres* (*Lives of Celebrated Spaniards*). The prince of the title was don Carlos, elder son of Juan II of Aragón and the half brother of the famous Ferdinand, future husband of Isabella the Catholic. At the time of the events of the play, 1460 and 1461, the prince has been summoned by his father to account for his participation in an uprising in the Kingdom of Navarre against his stepmother, the Queen doña Juana Enríquez. Although don Carlos was the rightful heir to the throne of Navarre through his mother, his father named his second wife as ruler through a loophole in the wording of the will. It is in the aftermath of this strife that the work opens as doña Juana overtly works for the destruction of her stepson.

The King don Juan is at first prepared to mitigate his anger against his son and to seek a just compromise to the situation, but the queen is determined to bring about the downfall of the prince. She tells the chancellor: "pues sé que nada, canciller, resiste / al gran querer de un ánimo resuelto" ("I know that nothing, chancellor, can resist / the strong will of a resolute spirit"), (*OB* II, 76). She plays on her husband's ego, saying that he is afraid of his son, that he is growing old and cowardly, and that he is denying the rights of his younger son. Her final trump is to point out the popularity of the prince who is being acclaimed in the courtyard below as he arrives. She declares, "Nunca objeto / fuisteis de tanto amor" ("Never were you the object of such love"), (*OB* II, 81). It is this that finally turns the king to anger: "¡Llegar a mi presencia como en triunfo, / cuando le llamo a responder cual reo!" ("To come into my presence in a state of triumph / when I call him to answer charges as a criminal!", (*OB* II, 82).

In the interview between father and son, the latter consistently shows his love and loyalty, while the king grows more and more frenzied and vindictive toward the son he accuses of having betrayed him to his enemies. Don Carlos knows that the poisonous tongue of his stepmother has brought about the situation. The king, implacable, orders his arrest. After the arrest, Isabel, daughter of the chancellor, confronts the queen with the seriousness of her actions, and when she is alone, gives a powerful verbal portrait of the queen in a soliloquy in which she admits her love for the prince. Her virtuous love and that of the prince for his father are the counterbalance to the jealousy and hatred of the queen. As daughter of the chancellor, Isabel can enter the tower prison of don Carlos. She tells him of the nobles' plans to save his life and gains his confidence. In his conversation with Isabel, the prince speaks of the sadness of the lot which destiny has brought him and of his life of isolation and solitude, themes dear to Tula in her other works that reflect her thoughts about her own life.

While Isabel is in the tower, her father arrives to tell the prince that the queen has come to speak with him. He sees that a woman is with the prince, and the latter tries to hide the fact that it is Isabel. He succeeds for only a moment, and so the daughter's honor is supposedly besmirched, recalling the false accusation against Fronilde in *Munio Alfonso,* and the unfounded gossip about Leoncia. The queen offers don Carlos his life in exchange for a renunciation of all rights to the throne, but the prince stands firm, vowing that he will die with honor. Meanwhile, armed forces come to liberate the prince are heard outside the castle. The chancellor draws his sword and challenges the prince, supposedly in defense of his honor as a father, but Isabel intervenes and soldiers lead don Carlos away.

In the final act, the troops of Catalunia and of Castille have been successful. Even the queen recognizes the futility of not acceding to their wishes for the prince's release. When this is finally carried out, don Carlos acts with noble dignity, forgiving his odious stepmother, and showing her public honor. His leave-taking of Isabel is affectionate and tender. After he has gone, the queen, thinking herself alone, reveals that she has poisoned her stepson and that he will soon fall dead. Isabel overhears doña Juana and accuses her of her crime. The king enters, and Isabel declares the infamous act of the queen to him, as word is brought that the prince has fallen dead as he left the castle. Isabel, cursing the queen for regicide and the father for filicide, takes her father's dagger and kills herself.

As a work, The *Prince of Viana* is less accomplished than *Munio Alfonso.* In many ways it is less so than *Leoncia.* The love affair between Isabel and don Carlos does not develop beyond devotion between a loyal subject and a grateful monarch. Even the queen does not quite become the hateful figure that la Avellaneda wished to make of her, a kind of medieval Medea. Neither the motivation nor the characterization is fully sustained, and it is undoubtedly because she recognized the defects of the drama that Tula did not include the play in the edition of *Obras completas* until the novelist Fernán Caballero urged her to change her mind. Neither the plight of don Carlos or of Isabel is sufficiently gripping to maintain our interest, while the queen and aging monarch are not of sufficient stature to arouse either pity or terror.

IV   Egilona

Egilona is another *drama trágico*. It is based on legendary material concerning don Rodrigo, the last of the Visigothic kings who was defeated by the invading Moorish armies in 711. The play is set in Seville in the year 715. Tula wrote that she had completed the work in a scant three days and did not think it worthy of inclusion in the volumes of dramas of the *Obras completas* of 1869. It was, however, included in the centenary edition of 1914. The work follows the tradition of historical tragedy that the authoress had utilized in the plays discussed above. Here she takes pseudohistorical material and fills it out with her own imaginings and invention.

Several playwrights had treated the story of Egilona, Rodrigo's wife who supposedly survived him, and of her marriage to the Moorish Emir Abdelasis. Probably la Avellaneda took the core of her story from Mariana or Conde who tell of the death of the emir. Gertrudis, unlike the others who used the same tale, has Rodrigo survive the battle in which he was defeated and confront the emir and his supposed widow after the latter has already remarried. This greatly increases the complexity of plotting, at which la Avellaneda is very skilled, but does place the work clearly in the romantic school rather than the neoclassical. The plot lines and dramatic tensions are weakened by the overabundance of incident, becoming confusing and tangential.

The play was composed at a particularly confused period of la Avellaneda's life, and it may well be this that the author has unwittingly projected into her drama. In 1844, when she drafted the play, she had begun her unhappy love affair with the poet Tassara, which was to end with the birth and tragic loss of a daughter. Cepeda was still in the background of her thoughts and emotions, and, ironically, the postponed opening of *Egilona* took place while Tula and her first husband, Sabater, were in Paris for the tracheotomy that would make a widow of her. Even the production of the play seemed fated for disappointment. The actors of Tula's choice were not able to do the roles, and the timing of the opening, June, was poorly chosen for a serious drama. It seemed as though the fate of which the author so often spoke had worked its worst. In the dedication of the play to the actress Barbara Lamadrid, who had played the Empress Berenguela in *Munio Alfonso* and Queen Juana in *The Prince of Viana,* and who was to have played the starring role of Egilona, Gertrudis speaks of her own talent as weakened "by the irritating and tenacious illness that has been attacking my nerves and brain for some time now."[12]

One thing that marks the major characters, a reflection of the state of nerves of the author, is their moments of frenzy and near madness. Whether an expression of love, of defiance, of anger, or of jealousy, the excesses of emotion that border on insanity are relieved only by passages of considerable lyrical beauty. On the positive side, the mastery of dialogue, of versification, and of plot was something which even adverse critics were quick to recognize.

As the play opens, Caleb, captain of the emir's guard, expresses envy for his master's happiness and power and the hatred which he, a Berber conquered by the Arabs, feels toward Abdelasis. His rancor has been increased by the marriage of Abdelasis that night to the beautiful Christian widow of the defeated Visigothic king, don Rodrigo. Caleb also loves Egilona, and his jealousy and envy make of him an Iago determined to destroy the master whom he pretends to serve but whom he betrays at every opportunity. Caleb is the figure of evil, reminiscent of the seducer in la Avellaneda's poetry, of Fernando in *Leoncia,* and of the queen in *El príncipe de Viana*. He inextricably snares the principal characters in a net of violent death, provoking the destruction of all their hopes and virtuous intentions.

Abdelasis, despite moments of threatened violence, rivals the prince of Viana in nobility of soul. Deeply and tenderly in love with Egilona, he is generous toward the defeated Christians. His virtues, however, are powerless in the face of the treachery of Caleb, who turns even the emir's trusted friend against him, saying that he has betrayed his own people and his religion by his marriage to a Christian. Egilona also is virtuous. Although she believes herself to be a widow, she is deeply troubled by her marriage to Abdelasis and has a disturbing vision of Rodrigo. When, in the dungeon where he is held captive, Rodrigo appears before her eyes, she cannot believe that he is real. Once that fact is established, however, Egilona recognizes that her duty is to her first husband, despite her love for the second. When, at the end of the play, Abdelasis is murdered in the mosque, Egilona remains with him, villifying his killers and taking her own life by his side. Rodrigo survives and is fighting once more against the Moors as the work ends.

The inclusion of the return of Rodrigo—a detail invented by Gertrudis and not found in other versions of the story of Egilona and Abdelasis—makes two dramas in one, first, that of the love story of the widow and the emir and their struggle for happiness in the face of the political, social, and religious obstacles that threaten to overwhelm them, and second, the problem of Egilona as lover newlywed to one man while still the wife of another whom she had thought dead. Either story would conceivably have sufficed for the drama, and although the figure of Rodrigo is an admirable one—strong, determined, noble—the relationships are never quite clearly worked out. Egilona's feeling and her loyalties are divided and despite the finality of her decision to die at Abdelasis's side, thereby reflect the confused and troubled period through which the author herself was passing as she wrote the drama.

V Saul

The first version of the biblical drama *Saul* was written in

1844 and was known in manuscript form at the same time as *The Prince of Viana.* La Avellaneda had read two earlier versions of the story in dramatic form, plays by the Italian Alfieri (1782), and by the French playwright Alexandre Soumet (1822). She had begun a translation of the latter, but gave it up, deciding to write her own original version of the drama.[13] She abandoned the unities of the French play, and although she first wrote the work in five acts, later changed this to four. Taking it with her to Paris in 1845, she showed it to friends there, but not until May, 1849, did the work open in Madrid at the newly renovated Teatro Español. While not a great popular success, the critics gave it high praise; the production itself was remarkable for its sumptuousness, and the royal family and the highest figures of social and artistic circles came to applaud the work and its author. It was, and still is, considered one of la Avellaneda's masterworks.

In a prologue written for presentation at a reading of the play before the Madrid *Liceo*, Gertrudis tells of her reading of Alfieri and Soumet, but states that she feels that she has succeeded in giving more movement and more *drama* to the biblical story than her predecessors. She observes that the story of Saul was one that she had long consideded especially appropriate for a drama, for she conceived overweening pride as a theme eminently suited for tragedy, a subject capable of exciting terror and piety. She also claims, and rightly so, that she has faithfully followed the story as outlined in the Scriptures. What she does embroider and expand upon is the love story of David and Micol. For their scenes together she writes lyrical poetry quite worthy of standing on its own. She also utilizes the theme of David's harp to assert her ideas on creativity and poetry, the same ones that we find in the poems of her published collections. When the music of the harp sounds within the temple before which Micol and her friend Sela stand in anticipation of the victory celebration over the Amelecites, the latter comments: "se dice / que al son de su arpa los dolores cesan. / y que huyen los espíritus malignos / del infeliz mortal en quien se albergan" ("it is said / that at the sound of his harp all pain ceases, / and malign spirits flee / from the unhappy mortal in which they take refuge"), (*OB* II, 222). In a later passage, as the love between

David and Micol grows, the themes of music—and thereby poetry as a gift of God—is reintroduced, as well as the concept that the beauty of nature is fleeting, while that of art is lasting. This contrasts with the following scene in which the sacriligeous Saul takes the corrupted first fruits of his victory to the altars. This he does in express defiance of God's commands given to the king by the priest Achimelich and the prophet Samuel. Divine wrath at Saul's action is evident in the growing storm and in the lightning that illuminates the sky as Samuel appears to warn the king against his sacrilege. The prophet calls Saul "rebelde, impío" ("rebel, impious"), and accuses him: "te apropias del maldito las riquezas; / del sacerdocio abates los derechos" ("you appropriate the riches of the damned; / of the priesthood you abase the rights"), (OB II, 230).

The story line is, of course, familiar to any reader of the Bible. Samuel prophesies that Saul's throne will go to someone not of his blood. Saul's nights are filled with horrifying dreams and fearful visions. He promises the hand of his daughter Micol to the victor over Goliath. It is David who goes forth to triumph over the giant and the Philistines, and Jonathan recounts the victory. David's humility when he appears victorious before his king is in striking contrast to the prideful attitude of Saul. David states that he has always lived without ambition ("siempre he vivido a la ambición ajeno"), (OB II, 250). It is at this point that David infers the coming of the Christ who will be the conquering monarch of the universe.

At this point, and just before the wedding of David and Micol, news of Samuel's impending death is brought to Saul. The messenger repeats the prophecy that his scepter will go to a humble native of Bethlehem, whereupon Saul orders Abner to go to the temple to find and kill David. David escapes as Johathan and Micol protest their father's unjust and cruel sentence, thereby incurring his wrath. Samuel appears to Saul, whose death decree against the Levites further increases his damnation. The monarch forces the Pythoness of Endor to come to him to predict the future, and despite her protests that he should renounce his fatal curiosity, finally reveals to him that he will kill both himself and his hopes for the future. The vision of the spirit of Samuel increases Saul's madness, and in the ultimate act of frenzy he kills the man who wears David's helmet: his own son Jonathan. Saul thus commits filicide, and, subsequently takes his own life. Achimelech the priest takes the dead monarch's crown and places it on David's head.

A look at the elements that the story involves, and that Tula introduces, produces a compendium of themes and situations already utilized in the plays discussed. There is no "triangle" in the love affair, but the changing stances of Saul prevent love's real fulfillment. The loyalty of the son, Jonathan, is unjustly rejected by Saul. Both children, Jonathan and Micol, are the type of innocent and virtuous youths that appear in all of la Avellaneda's plays. Saul represents murder and suicide, as well as the embodiment of evil and of madness. His antagonist, David, symbolizes humble strength, virtuosity, and the poetic soul touched by divine grace. Samuel and the Pythoness of Endor add the touches of the mysterious and the exotic so dear to the romantic psyche. Ritual scenes permit the use of music and of spectacle to break the high seriousness of the subject matter, and the final triumph of David raises the ending above the violence and death in the killings of Jonathan and Saul on stage.

VI Recaredo

Recaredo, or *Flavio Recaredo* as the play was originally entitled, is set in Visigothic Spain. Designated simply as a *drama* in three acts, it is written in a wider variety of meters than the previous works in verse. Although composed two years earlier, the play was not produced until October 27, 1851. The time of the action is around ,586 A.D. The historical events which form the background of the play are part of the struggles between Suevians and Visigoths, on one level, and between the heresy of Aryanism and Papal Catholicism on another. The Recaredo of the title is an Aryan, the son of King Leovigildo. Leovigildo had dethroned and persecuted his predecessor, whose daughter, Bada, the major female character of the drama, lives humbly in Mérida. Her mother has died shortly before the action of the play begins. Bada is dressed in mourning, and her opening speech clearly links her to the author in theme and content. Bada identifies herself as an exile from her native soil—thus, Tula

far from her beloved Cuba—and an orphan without protection,
i.e., the Tula who lost her father at age nine: "mas hoy a la
huérfana triste, / sin patria, ni arrimo, ni hogar, / por toda
existencia le queda, / rencor en el alma . . . y no más!" ("but
today the unhappy orphan / without country or protection or
home, / for all of her existence still has / only ill will in her
soul . . . and nothing more!"), (*OB* II, pp. 143–44). The bitterness is obviously the rancor that stems from the deeply dis-
illusioning events of the love affair with Tassara, the loss of
Brenhilde, and then the death of Sabater. Tula consequently
identifies herself with the princess and her vicissitudes.

Viterico, a page of Duke Claudio, and also an orphan, declares his love for Bada, and in the hopes of winning her favor,
promises to help her find vengeance against Recaredo and the
Aryan heresy. Sunna, an Aryan priest, comes to tell Bada of a
conspiracy to do away with Recaredo. He gives an exposition
of the background of the problems, and upon Viterico's asking
who is the head of the conspirators, names Agrimundo—the king's
chamberlain and favorite. Sunna says that although no royal
blood runs in Agrimundo's veins, he has the heart of a hero
and is deserving of the crown. Bada, however, calls both men
blasphemers after they have gone and says that she cannot be
a part of their conspiracy.

At this point, the Archbishop Mausona comes to offer consolation to Bada on the loss of her mother. He offers her even more,
a protector and a "father." When Bada asks the name of this
man, Mausona replies that she should call him Agrimundo and
that he has confidence in the great man whom she is about to
meet. As Mausona leaves the room, it is Recaredo and not Agrimundo who encounters him. The king asks what name he is to
use. Mausona replies that it is Agrimundo. Therefore, it is as
the king's chamberlain that Bada receives him, not as the king.
The ensuing dialogue, in which Recaredo's love is awakened
and in which he swears to bring about the religious and political
unity that Bada so fervently wishes, contains a spiritual self-
portrait of la Avellaneda, lonely, apprehensive, and embittered.
Viterico observes a man leave Bada's room, but does not know
who he is.

At the end of the meeting, Sunna arrives with word that the

king of France has begun an invasion against Recaredo, and that
Viterico and Agrimundo are to murder Recaredo and Duke
Claudio. Viterico, however, remains with Bada to demand that
she promise him her hand in marriage. Otherwise he will reveal
the conspiracy and "Agrimundo's" part in it. Viterico, the jealous
and unworthy suitor willing to sell his services for his own
advantage, is incapable of comprehending either Bada's or
Recaredo's greatness of soul. The real Agrimundo is also a traitor
who, despite his privileges and the favor shown to him by his
royal master, is prepared, like a latter-day Macbeth, to kill his
sovereign. Bada, however, sees "Agrimundo" as the potential
savior of her country and her religion, and Recaredo as the embodiment of all that is vile and reprehensible. Consequently,
mistaken identity is fundamental to the development of the plot.

In the second act, there occurs a revelation scene between
Agrimundo and Viterico. The latter declares his jealousy, and the
former tells him that it was Recaredo and not he who had talked
with Bada. When the duke interrupts the conversation, Viterico
is confused, unable to do more than convey the news of the
French invasion. The duke gives Viterico his sword, and this
sign of honor leaves Viterico perturbed and undecided. His sense
of decency finally triumphs, as Recaredo enters and talks with
the duke and Mausona. As the king retires, Agrimundo prepares
his dagger to kill him while Bada pounds at the door. Recaredo
himself responds and sees the dagger which Agrimundo has let
fall. Bada has come to warn "Agrimundo" that the conspiracy
will be denounced. She tells Recaredo of the plans, so that the
treachery of the real Agrimundo is thereby revealed, just as the
duke and Mausona arrive to protect their sovereign. Bada won-
ders if what she is witnessing is a dream.

Recaredo's clemency in dealing with the traitors earns the
admiration of all and strengthens Bada's love for him. There
is, however, a sudden reversal of situation when the king tells
Bada that she must pay for the crime of participation in the
conspiracy. She is left in the power of Mausona to whom she
confesses her true crime as being that of her heart. This she also
confesses in the last act, set in Toledo, to her confidante, Erme-
senda, as she declares: "mientras le execran los labios, / el
pecho, amiga, le adora" ("while my lips execrate him, / my

breast, my friend, adores him"), (*OB* II, 196). It is in this
scene in which Bada expresses the inner conflict between her
love and her concept of duty to her people, her duty to avenge
her father and her adherence to Catholicism, as la Avellaneda
parallels the struggles of Corneille's Chimène. Her love is insane,
and because of the abyss which separates her from Recaredo and
of her oath to become a nun, she is without hope. Recaredo,
however, returns victorious to find his "dulce enemigo" ("sweet
enemy"), (*OB* II, 202), and shows Bada the decree that he has
signed which unites Spain to the Holy Catholic Church of Rome.
He declares his love, but is rebuffed, first for the acts of his
father against Bada's family and her people, and finally by her
vow. Mausona, however, releases Bada from her vow so that the
pair can be married. Recaredo's final speech foreshadows the
carrying of Christianity to the New World.

Complicated in its plotting and its structure and obscure in
the historical period in which it was set—even for a Spanish
audience of la Avellaneda's day—the play nevertheless contains
excellent passages of dialogue and of lyric beauty. The love
scenes between Recaredo and Bada and the moments of intro-
spection on the part of the latter give the work moments of
lasting interest.

VII   La verdad vence apariencias

The opening of *La verdad vence apariencias* (*Truth Van-
quishes Appearances*) in Madrid on January 22, 1852, marked
the beginning of la Avellaneda's production of dramas less
serious in tone than the tragedies that she had written up to this
time. It also was the first of five plays to open in the same year,
four of which were successes. The play was finished by December, 1851, at which time Tula had a reading before a group
of literary friends and admirers. The work is adapted from a
play of Byron's, *Werner*, which in turn the English poet had
taken from a novel by Harriet Lee, *The German's Tale Kruitzner*.
Both previous works were set in Germany, and the characters
of the macabre and complex story were all German. The time
was the seventeenth century during the Thirty Years Wars.

La Avellaneda did no more than take the skeleton of the plot, and may well be said to have so completely transformed the tale, changing time, place and characters, as to make it completely new. Tula sets her work in Spain at the time of the Battle of Nájera in 1367, and three years later. All of the characters of the story are Spanish, and one of them at least—King Enrique III— is historical. Something remains of the Gothic tale in the involved and unsavory story of changed and mistaken identity, fratricidal hatreds, murder, and injustice, but despite the seriousness of the subject matter, Gertrudis does maintain something of a light touch. This play is classed as a drama, not tragic drama as are the earlier works. There is even a note of humor in the rustic conversation of two of the servants, a device which Tula utilized with frequency in her *comedias*. The dark secret corridor of the castle in which the prologue takes place becomes symbolic of the labyrinthine mystery of personalities and of their deeds—for the play is a mystery story—and the identity of the murderer remains undivulged until the very end.

The basic theme is fratricidal jealousy and hatred. Don Tello has usurped his brother's rights. The brother, don Alvaro, has taken refuge in a castle under an assumed name, Beltrán. His younger son Rodrigo is with him. His elder son was kidnapped in infancy and his whereabouts is unknown. The night of the Battle of Nájera, don Tello, the evil brother, is brought wounded into the castle. A young man, Fernán, who saved the noble's life is with him, offering to stay by the wounded man's side during the night. Fernán had earlier been sent away from don Tello's household. A servant reveals that don Tello's young daughter had become enamored of Fernán, and for this reason the father had banished him. Rodrigo leaves the castle to go into the village, and a warrior enters asking refuge of Beltrán.

The voices of the keepers of the castle are heard, announcing that the gates are to be closed. Beltrán offers to tell the Aragonese warrior of a secret passageway that leads either to the outside or into the bedchamber where don Tello lies. As the warrior is from the losing side of don Enrique, Don Tello is his enemy. Entering the passageway, he subsequently reappears covered with blood. After his escape, the keeper of the castle finds don Tello murdered and accuses Fernán of the killing. Beltrán protects him, exhibiting a document proving that he is in reality don Alvaro, the brother of the murdered man and rightful heir to the title.

The remaining two acts of the play take place three years later, on the anniversary of the crime. Leonor, daughter of the late don Tello and the niece of don Alvaro, is betrothed to Rodrigo, but does not love him, and he is aware of this. Leonor confesses to her confidante that it was Fernán whom she loved, despite the latter's humble origins. At this point, Fernán appears, posing as a page and telling Leonor of his adventures since he fled. The love of the two is evident, but the love story is complicated briefly when Fernán shows Leonor a locket with a picture of her mother in it, bearing the family coat of arms. Fernán tells Leonor that his supposed father had sworn to him on his deathbed that the locket was from his true family. Supposedly, they, like Carlos and Elena of *Leoncia*, are half-brother and sister and can never marry. Don Alvaro recognizes the locket and declares Fernán to be none other than his long-lost son Gonzalo, the elder of his two boys. Rodrigo, however, accuses Gonzalo of the murder of don Tello and has him imprisoned. The king arrives for the projected wedding of Leonor and Rodrigo—the same Enrique who had lost the battle three years before —and don Alvaro recognizes the warrior from Aragon who had entered the secret corridor, whom he believes to be the true murderer. The king, however, knows the true killer to be Rodrigo. To save don Alvaro's honor, he sends the guilty brother off to fight the Portuguese and the Moors, thus resolving the play in the same way as *Munio Alfonso*, and leaving Gonzalo and Leonor to marry.

VIII   Errores del corazón

The next play of la Avellaneda's to be produced was *Errores del Corazón* (*Errors of the Heart.*) Her first "comedy" (i.e., drama reasonably light in tone and content), it opened in Madrid on May 7, 1852, and was a modest success. It was written in prose rather than in verse, no doubt considered more fitting for a work set in Tula's own times rather than the historically remote epochs of the other plays (excepting *Leoncia*). The work may be classified as a "sentimental comedy" and is based on a kind of love situation, already very popular in such Golden Age playwrights as Lope de Rueda or Moreto, in which A loves B, but B loves C, and so on. It was not included either in the *Obras completas* of 1869 or in the Centennial edition of 1914, and is generally accepted as fundamentally autobiographical. Many of the declarations of love, whether passionate or unselfish, may be traced to the autobiographical writings of Tula and to the love letters.

Doctor Román is a kind and thoughtful man, aged forty-five, always helping others, who has brought a poor foundling, María, into his home and cared for her. He has cured the Countess Valsano of tuberculosis, and has made his young nephew Fernando's fortune. María falls in love with her benefactor; the doctor falls in love with the countess, and she, in turn, with Fernando. The latter, egotistical and materialistic, loves only himself, but agrees to marry the countess when his uncle settles half of his fortune on him. María, seeing the suffering of don Román and knowing the fickle character of Fernando, speaks with the countess on behalf of the benefactor she herself loves. In the interim, don Román has decided to leave the capital and to retire to a farm, making María his chief heir. First María, and then the doctor, fall ill from emotional reaction to these situaitons. María nurses her friend back to health.

The doctor, deciding that to pursue an impossible ideal in the countess is unrealistic, takes María to a ball at the countess' home. The countess also has had a change of heart, having learned that Fernando had courted her sister during her illness. This, coupled with María's earlier advice to marry don Román, accounts for her changing her mind. She will accept the doctor's hand, but he recognizes the fact that she does not love him and would only be sacrificing herself for his happiness were she to marry him.

Contemporary critics found the character of the doctor, the man in middle age who had previously repressed all emotional and physical passion, of particular interest. The figure of María also generated certain interest. Fundamentally a romantic heroine, she is virtuous and innocent, sacrificing herself for the man she loves. Fernando is a type of selfish dandy that we know existed in the epoch. His loss of the countess's hand and her fortune was not only an "error of the heart," but a serious financial setback. His is the greatest loss, but it was he who gave the least to others.

IX El donativo del diablo

The third play produced in 1852, *El donativo del diablo* (*The Gift of the Devil*), opened in October to a fairly good reception by the public, but was unfavorably reviewed by the critics. The play was a dramatization of the novella, *La velada del helecho, o el donativo del diablo* (*The Vigil of the Fern Plant, or the Gift of the Devil*) which la Avellaneda had published in 1849. The story was based on a Swiss folktale that Tula's brother, Manuel, told her after a trip to Switzerland, which is where the action is set, in the fourteenth century.

Several elements would have attracted Gertrudis to this tale, including first of all the frustrated love situation of Arnaldo and Ida. The young page of the count of Montsalvens has no background and no fortune, so that Ida's father repudiates the possible match. Arnaldo is an orphan whose family antecedents are unknown, but he, like the girl he loves, is virtuous and innocent. He is willing, however, to do anything for love, and becomes a youthful Faust, prepared to sell his very soul to the devil in order not to lose the woman he loves.

The "gift of the devil" is the folktale that is central to the development of the plot. A belief existed that on the night of Saint John, a pact could be made with the devil. The fearful but determined Arnaldo goes to the designated spot and in the misty night hears a voice that tells him that he has come there for the love of a woman. He is given certain conditions—not the selling of his soul as he had expected—for getting the money needed to obtain Ida's hand. He must take from the count a coffer with a coat of arms on its lid and bring it back two or three nights later. Arnaldo has easy access to the coffer and does take it. The "devil" has assured him that he had full right to take it as it rightfully belonged to him. Arnaldo is arrested for the robbery, first of the money which the "devil" had given to him, and for the taking of the coffer.

In the dungeon where he is imprisoned for the theft, Arnaldo

tells his tale to Ida. The count appears and threatens the innocent lovers with torture to the death unless they reveal the whereabouts of the coffer. At this point, the Baron de Charmey enters
to disclose the importance of the papers that the coffer held.
Arnaldo and the baron are half brothers, the former the result
of an illicit love affair of their mother. The count, who had treated
Arnaldo like a servant, had been left a large inheritance for the
child. The baron denounces the count, and promises protection
for the newly found brother whom he had tricked into stealing
the coffer by posing as the Devil on Saint John's Eve.

Adverse criticism of this play did not prevent Tula from presenting others for production, and yet another work opened in
Madrid in October.

X La hija de las flores o todos están locos

On October 21, 1852, *La hija de las flores o todos están locos*
(*The Daughter of the Flowers or Everybody's Crazy*) opened to
resounding public and critical success. A work in three acts and
in verse, it is designated by its author as a *comedia original*. The
play does contain comical elements, but the seriousness of much
of its subject matter places it more in the category of straight
drama. The story, although handled with a light touch, basically
concerns serious matters with both social and moral implications.

We might say that *The Daughter of the Flowers* is *Leoncia*
rewritten with a happy ending, as various themes of Tula's first
play reappear in this one. A marriage has been arranged between
a young man named Luis and Inés, an older woman. Neither one
wants the marriage, but both agree to it in deference, respectively, to an uncle and a father. It is, consequently, a loveless
match that is being imposed on Luis and Inés through social
custom and material pressures. Don Luis is submissive to his
uncle, the count of Mondragon. Inés is also submissive, but
strangely withdrawn in all social contact. We presumably know
Luis's character, but we do not know Inés: mystery envelopes
her.

The third figure of what becomes a triangle is Flora, the
"daughter of the flowers," whose identity is even more mysterious than that of Inés. She is too lovely and aristocratic to

be the child of Tomasa and Juan, rustic housekeepers of the country estate at which the action takes place. She even seems too highly born to be the offspring of Beatriz, nurse and companion to Inés. Flora herself insists that she is the daughter of the flowers in the garden, and that she had no father. Like the flowers, she is beautiful and carefree, innocent, guileless, and artless in her beauty. When don Luis meets her, he is transformed by his love for her. He wants freedom from the shackles which his uncle has prepared for him.

The life of seclusion which Inés has lived has not gone without comment in Madrid, although she lived in Valencia rather than with her father in the capital. The rumor is that she is insane, and the strangeness of her conversations with Luis seems to bear this out. She makes it clear to her reluctant fiancé that she is no more desirous of the wedding than he is. Meanwhile Luis's actions become more and more erratic. No one knows of Flora's presence but Luis. Even Tomasa thinks that she has her safely locked away from the visiting guests, and consequently, Luis also is suspected of madness. Flora speaks to him with the voice of nature and simple truth. She asks Luis how he can say he loves her and still plan to marry another woman. He explains that this is happening because of a tyrannical obligation, because of the force of people's opinion. When Flora suggests that they flee from such a situation, Luis speaks with the voice of the man conditioned by society. How could they live? he asks, and the innocent Flora replies that Nature lives through God's grace, and so could they.

Events take a sudden turn when Luis gives a *fleur de lis* to Inés; upon seeing the flower, she becomes almost mad, faints, and must be taken away by Beatriz. Her father orders that the flowers of the garden be destroyed to avoid further possibility of exciting Inés' mania. Thus, Luis is mad in his love of flowers, and Inés mad in her reaction to them. The flowers are the creators of this madness, while the *fleur de lis* is somehow the key to its solution. The count, after seeing Inés' reaction to the lily, pounds his forehead with his fist, recalling something hidden in his memory about just such a lily. He too meets and talks with Flora, is charmed by her and says that he, too, is going mad.

In the final act, Inés confides to the count the secret of the lily. One day while visiting an aunt in the country, she had dropped a lily into a stream. Leaning over to recover the flower, she had fallen in and would have drowned had not a young hunter rescued her, unconscious, from the water. When she had come to, lying under a tree, she found a lily on her breast and a note saying: "Consérvala por recuerdo / de mi rápida ventura . . ." ("Keep this in memory / of my brief happiness . . ."), (*OB* III, 99). The hunter who had seduced Inés eighteen years before was none other than the count himself, and Flora their natural daughter. The count reveals to Inés that the daughter that she had been told was dead is very much alive and in that very house. Unlike the hunter-seducer of *Leoncia*, however, there is no sense of restitution, as marriage will ultimately erase the count's evil deed.

After a brief plot complication in which Flora is to be sent off to the New World, from which Luis rescues her, there is a happy ending. Inés will marry the man who had raped her and to whom she belongs by age as well as the fact that he is the father of her child. Luis will marry Flora to whom he belongs by love, age, and temperament.

In addition to the plot, the play offers much to entertain an audience. Flora has ample opportunity to recite some movingly lyrical poetry on the beauties of flowers and of nature, passages that rank with the best of Tula's lyrical poems. Humorous passages spark the dialogue of Tomasa and Juan, and occur between the count and the baron as they try unsuccessfully to fathom the "madness" of the happenings around them. Tula had once more proven her versatility; her comedy was a brilliant success. Gertrudis herself was feted with flowers the night of the triumphal opening.

XI La aventurera

The next play of la Avellaneda's, produced in 1853, and entitled *La aventurera* (*The Adventuress*), was an adaptation of a play of the same title by the French playwright Emile Augier. The French play was set in Padua in the seventeenth century, but Tula sets her play in Seville, some time after 1821. All of the characters are given Spanish names. Like the French model, *The Adventuress* is written in verse, but has four acts instead of five.

It is easy enough to see why la Avellaneda chose to adapt this particular play, for it contains themes dear to her heart: the sinful woman; the "adventuress" who is virtuous and decent despite past transgressions; the young couple whose marriage plans seem thwarted; and not only one but two men who fit the category of evil seducers. Natalia and her so-called "brother" the marquis clearly belong to the picaresque world of adventurers and swidlers. Eduardo, the son of the widower, don Julián, who wishes to marry Natalia, is the prodigal son who returns. He tells his sister that he is older in spirit than in body, when he comes home so changed physically that he is able to fool even his father into thinking that he is a friend of his son's, and somewhat older than the son would have been. He soon sees Natalia and the marquis for what they are, and tricks the latter into admitting the truth. He also endeavors to trick Natalia, and would have succeeded had she not sincerely decided to act openly and honestly in her search for decency and the effacing of her past.

Significantly, Natalia confesses to don Julián of her own volition that she and the marquis are not ruined aristocrats fleeing the Independence of Mexico as they pretended to be. Natalia, who has neither name nor family, was an orphan whose youthful beauty and innocence were exploited by a man she calls a "monster." What she sought in the marriage to don Julián was not his money, but a name, peace, the happiness of a home, and to be loved with a chaste and pure love: "Era, don Julián, un nombre! / Era la paz, la ventura / de su doméstico hogar, / y el gozo de verme amar / con afección casta y pura." (*OB* III, 146–47). When don Julián asks Natalia why she had lied to him about herself, she replies simply and honestly that she had feared that he would follow the dictates of the world and condemn her. He recognizes the truth in this and says: "¡Oh necias leyes sociales! / son origen de mil males ... / mas ¿quién rompe su cadena?" ("Oh stupid social laws! / they are the origin of a thousand evils... / but who can break their chain?"), (*OB* III, 147). As this scene represents an important change made by la

Avellaneda from the French original, we can see it—and the confrontations which are to take place further on between Eduardo, whose dishonesty has been found out, and the nobility of Natalia, whom he persists in vilifying—as Tula's own defense against the implacable gossip that plagued her. It was in 1853 that the episode of the Royal Spanish Academy took place, and that la Avellaneda had to undergo severe public criticism, some of it, as in the "doña Sappho" lampoon, with unpleasant undertones.[14] Natalia's longing for a home and a kind and loving husband must similarly have been much on Tula's mind. Within less than two years after the production of this play, her last illusions were gone. She married Colonel Verdugo and had to undergo, in the attack on him, even greater sorrow.

Natalia solves her plight by giving her money for the care of orphans like herself and by retiring to a convent, a solution likewise in Tula's thoughts, as she wrote to Cepeda that she was considering such a move at just about this time. The play's pervading cynicism rings truer than the contrived happy ending which seems very much out of place. Natalia's sacrifice allows the young couple, Luisa and Carlos, to realize their hopes of marriage, and through their joy, don Julián is rapidly and miraculously reconciled to the loss of Natalia, something which no pleading or arguments could do before. Eduardo's transformation is equally unconvincing. He will devote his life to humanity, his implacable hatred of Natalia having been changed to love.

La Aventurera is of interest not in terms of the quality or accuracy of the translation and transposition, but for the light the work sheds on la Avelleneda's attitudes and feelings in a crucial moment in her art and her life.

A week after the opening of this play, a second translation from the French by la Avellaneda was produced. Entitled *Hortensia*, it was adapted from the play of the same name by the French playwright Frederick Soulié. Tula did not have the play printed, and so our only knowledge of the Spanish version comes through newspaper reviews. This work also contained the theme of seduction, and a series of love letters were read into the dialogue. Hortensia, like Natalia, is caught between actions of the past and their effect on the present and the future. The production lasted on stage only a few days.

The same was to happen to an original play of Tula's that opened on March 4, 1854. Written in five acts in prose, it was entitled *La somnámbula* (*The Sleepwalker*), and lasted just three days. The reviews were sharply critical, and probably for this reason Gertrudis did not have the play printed. Critics described it as lacking in verisimilitude, and even as lacking in taste. Tula had succeeded in softening the fundamental cynicism of *The Adventuress* by adding a highly improbable virtuous ending, but reviewers stated their disapproval of the depiction of vice on the stage. Although the play only gently hints at what Natalia's early life must have been, the heroine's decision to enter a convent and the hero's to devote his life to "humanity" apparently sufficed to satisfy public and critical opinion. La Avellaneda's subsequent, realistic treatment of a crime and of the materialism of society in *The Sleepwalker* was too far ahead of its time. A certain idealism, a moral ending, was a necessary ingredient for success. *The Sleepwalker* failed, and like *Hortensia*, seems to have been lost to posterity.

XII Two One-Act Plays

In 1855, la Avellaneda saw three of her plays produced. Two were one-act works, *Simpatía y antipatía* (*Amity and Aversion*) and *La hija del rey René* (*The Daughter of King Rene*). Both were written in verse. The first play was possibly based on an eighteenth-century French work, and the second was a free translation of a drama by Gustave Lemoine. Gertrudis merely calls the work an *arreglo* or adaptation from the French. She included the latter work in the volume of *Obras completas* but excluded the other one.

The theme of *Amity and Aversion* is once again forced marriage. At the insistence of an aged guardian, a young couple are married. They had known each other as young children and had a strong aversion to each other. When the marriage takes place, the groom does not appear, but is represented by a proxy. As soon as the guardian dies, the husband sets out for Rome to obtain a divorce, but the couple meet, not knowing their true identities, and fall in love. After some minor plot complications, the truth comes out and the divorce plans, naturally, are forgotten.

The interest of the play lies in several statements revealing sentiments of the author. It is obviously Tula herself who speaks when the young wife Isabel states that "venturosos los que encuentran / de la vida en los umbrales / al ser que a su ser completa" ("happy are those who find early in their lives a being whose being completes their own"), (*OB* III, 340). On the matter of divorce, Isabel says that a union that has been sanctioned by the church can end only in the tomb. The count, however, contradicts this, affirming that "entre seres que se odian / no hay unión ni pudo haberla" ("between beings who hate each other / there is no union, nor can there be any"), (*OB* III, 341).

The Daughter of King René offered Tula a good opportunity for exhibiting her talents at versification, duly singled out by the critics for praise, but the play also contains several themes dear to her: love, beauty, and nature. The story concerns Yolanda, the daughter of King René, who has been blind from birth, but does not know that she is blind, as her father and her nurse-companion, María, have carefully protected her. She lives in a beautiful garden, and is, in a sense, another "daughter of the flowers." She, like Flora, is wholly untouched by the stains and soilings of the material world. To her, all is beauty in its pristine innocence.

The prince of Vaudemont climbs the wall into the garden, sees the princess and falls in love with her. He had seen Yolanda asleep on a bench in the garden and had kissed her hand, as he recounts to the Arabic physician, Ben Jahia, who had come to consult with the king about a cure for Yolanda's blindness. The prince manages to enter the garden again. Conversing with Yolanda, he tells her how beautiful she is, and compares her to the beauties of nature. He speaks in terms of color, and finds that the princess has never heard such concepts before. Happily, the doctor does cure the blindness and prince and princess will wed.

XIII   Oráculos de Talia o duendes en el palacio

The third play of 1855, which opened on March 15, was entitled *Oráculos de Talia o duendes en el palacio* (*Oracles of Thalia or Ghosts in the Palace*). Tula styled it a *comedia original* in five acts and in verse. The play, set in seventeenth-century Spain was probably inspired by Calderon de la Barca's play, *La dama duende*. The story is based on historical fact, the rise to power of don Fernando Valenzuela during King Carlos II's minority. The Valenzuela of history, not a particularly admirable character, gained the favor of the widow of Philip IV by keeping her informed of court gossip and intrigues. He reputedly also became the lover of the queen, Doña Mariana of Austria, who served as regent during her son's minority. The power struggle which ensued between her and Carlos II's bastard half-brother, don Juan, is incorporated into la Avellaneda's version of the story, wherein Valenzuela is highly idealized, a poet who rises to power through the efforts of the queen's lady-in-waiting, doña Eugenia. Valenzuela, who finally marries this lady, is also a playwright who rises to the highest political position, becoming prime minister and a grandee of Spain.

The Thalia of the title is a statue behind which doña Eugenia hides and through whom she speaks, recalling the talking head in Barcelona which astounded don Quixote. Eugenia also gathers information by hiding behind a secret door in the wall of Valenzuela's room, and thus becomes known as the *duende*, the ghost or spirit of the palace

The figure of Valenzuela was criticized by reviewers as being contradictory. The poet-playwright becomes a politician, but Tula does not show in him any of the qualities necessary for the change in station. While these criticisms are justifiable in the reading of the play, the interest of the work today resides in what it shows of la Avellaneda's attitudes and feelings when she wrote it. She obviously wanted to express her resentment over the refusal to admit her to the Royal Spanish Academy, which she attributed to politics and to intrigue. Her feelings are barely veiled in the play. The prologue which she wrote for the work does not mention the Academy, but the point of her declaration is clear. The artist should be judged on merit, and the minister should be named to his post for his ability; each person should find the way open for him to advance according to his talents and his efforts in the field in which he is most capable. He should not have to seek "por la intriga y el favor lo que no podía alcanzar por el mérito" ("through intrigue and favor what he could not obtain through merit"), (*OB* III, 204–5). La Avellaneda quotes one of Valenzuela's speeches to substantiate her point: "No soy genio universal: / ábranme campo en mi esfera, / y útil seré, grande / quizás" ("A universal genius I am not: / open up the way in my sphere, / and I shall be useful, even great / perhaps"). Consequently, the historical Valenzuela becomes of little interest, functioning as a vehicle for la Avellaneda to express her feelings about the state of art and the artist in a materialistic society where true vocation is stifled and talent unappreciated.

Not until 1858 did new plays of la Avellaneda appear in Madrid, but in that year two major works opened, one that was to affect her future deeply, and the other a great public triumph. The first, a comedy-drama, was *Three Loves*, and the second—a biblical tragedy whose success rivaled *Saul*—*Balthasar.*

XIV Tres amores

Critical or adverse reviews had made la Avellaneda sufficiently bitter to declare that she would not write for the theater again. Three years after the production of *Oracles of Thalia*, however, first a comedy and then a tragedy opened. *Tres amores* (*Three Loves*) was a drama in three acts and a prologue which premiered on March 20, 1858. As the title indicates, the major theme of love in three different manifestations provides la Avellaneda with the basic material for plot development and complication. Two major themes that we know were dear to la Avelleneda are woven into the story line of the woman protagonist: artistic creation, in the context of the world of playwrights and acting, and the thorny problem of a successful and talented woman having to choose between public fame and fortune and private happiness. Tula also utilized a series of motifs and devices which, as we have seen, constitute stock ingredients of her literary paraphernalia: the lovely and mysterious foundling; the young couple seemingly made for each other whose wedding plans go awry; innocence betrayed by a cynical, would-be seducer; family and social considerations that thwart love and fulfillment; and ambition, materialism, and egotism that almost triumph but which are vanquished by true feeling and virtue in the end. The prologue is primarily exposition which more properly should have been incorporated into the body of the three acts of the drama. The action takes place in the reign of Carlos III, in the second half of the eighteenth century, in a comfortable country house in the mountains of Navarre in northern Spain. Matilde, the central figure of the play, is of mysterious parentage. She has been brought up by a farm couple who act as caretakers, and whose son Antonio is deeply in love with their ward. The parents are hopeful that the deep affection between the two will be resolved in marriage. Matilde, however, has fallen in love with don Víctor de San Adrián, a playwright from Madrid who is a guest of the count of Lárraga, owner of the country house. San Adrián is attracted to the lovely young woman, but is too practical to become involved with her. He has ambitions to marry the daughter of Lárraga who will inherit the fortune and estates of her father and of his spinster sister. When he receives word that he has been appointed to a diplomatic post, he leaves, telling Matilde that she should marry Antonio, as her love could never fully satisfy him. Matilde, more than the innocent and rustic country girl that one might have expected, is determined, first of all, not to go into the convent to which her family has destined her, and second, to succeed in the very world where San Adrián has had his triumphs of art and love, the theater. Antonio resolves to flee with her.

The play proper begins five years after the events exposed in the prologue. Matilde has fully succeeded in her aim to become a famous actress, being—like la Avellaneda and the actresses who rose to fame in her plays—applauded, serenaded, and honored by an adoring public. She has taken the name of Celia, which San Adrián has ascribed to the ideal woman of his works, and is to appear in a tragedy written by him entitled *Sappho*. San Adrián returns to Madrid, and not recognizing Celia as the Matilde he had known in the country house, declares his love for her. In the intervening years, the count of Lárraga has lost his daughter, and San Adrián expects that he himself will be named heir to the count and his sister's fortune. What happens is quite different. When the count accidentally sees Matilde on the street, he believes her a reincarnation of his dead daughter, so striking is the resemblance.

It appears that Matilde and San Adrián are to be wed, but

again the playwright's cynical materialism triumphs over his feelings. He commits the tactical error of declaring his love for the spinster sister of the count, whom he mistakenly believes will be named heir to his estates. Meanwhile, the count has discovered the identity of Matilde. She is the daughter of his "spinster" sister who was married beneath her station to an artist whom she had loved in her youth. Count and sister declare Matilde to be their heir, and she, in her turn, decides to give her hand to the faithful and virtuous Antonio who had stayed loyally by her side—calling himself her brother—throughout all of her vicissitudes. The sensual love of San Adrián is rejected; the cerebral love of Matilde for San Adrián is exposed in its inadequacy; the true and persistent love of Antonio triumphs.

We may well speculate as to what extent Gertrudis is presenting composite portraits in the figures of San Adrián and Antonio, and to what degree words and names within the play are allusions to actual persons of the time. She may have been making veiled criticisms of hostile critics in the use of some names and situations, and this may have been a factor in the provoking of the "cat" incident described in chapter 1. Matilde's determination to win the love of San Adrián suggests la Avellaneda's own perseverance with Cepeda, while the figure of San Adrián in its materialism and cynical abandonment of the young woman imply that he is a composite portrait of Cepeda and of Tassara. By the time the play was produced, Tassara, like the San Adrián of the prologue, was on a diplomatic mission to the United States. The patient and loyal Antonio whom Matilde chooses as her husband and for whom she expresses affection but not real love, hints at the reality of both of Tula's marriages, and explains the ending of the play which critics of the time found fault with as unrealistic.

XV Baltasar

Baltasar, the last play of la Avellaneda's to be produced, and an incontestable triumph in the theater, had been completed at least two years before it opened in April 1858. The work is based on the biblical books of Daniel in which the story of Belshazzar's feast and the doom of the Kingdom of Babylon is briefly told. Whether Gertrudis drew on Byron's *Sardanapolis* for additional material to fill out her drama is uncertain. Probably she invented the story which culminates in the banquet scene of the vision of "Mene, Mene, Tekel, Upharsin" which Daniel interprets as foretelling the fall of Belshazzar's kingdom to the Medes.

Belshazzar (Baltasar) is portrayed as a corrupt and world-weary ruler, satiated with the pleasures of the senses, fawned upon and flattered by all who surround him, a victim of what Tula describes in the poem "Mi mal" ("My Torment") as tedium and a paralysis of will. The king, cognizant of his illness, calls it ennui or weariness ("fastidio"). He tells one of his ministers that he has struggled in vain to overcome it and that he recognizes that what he needs is a great passion ("alguna grande pasión"), some great love or hate, or revenge, some great pleasure or some great suffering ("Dame un placer, o un pesar / digno de esta alma infinita"). La Avellaneda, consequently, makes of Belshazzar a type of romantic hero, partially satanic, a figure whose innate capacity for greatness of feeling has been frustrated through his own and his courtiers' excesses, and who is doomed to suffer anguish and destruction. He is the exalted monarch, the hollow colossus, embodiment of the vanities of this world that will be reduced to dust.

The plot centers on the character of a beautiful young Jewess named Elda, niece of the prophet Daniel. She is engaged to Rubén, grandson of Jehoiachin (Joaquín), the last king of Judah who had been brought in captivity to Babylon by Belshazzar's father, Nebuchadnezzar. Despite their enslavement, neither Elda nor Rubén nor the aged Joaquín have lost their defiant spirit. When the Queen-Mother Nitocris takes Elda from her prison to appear before her son at a great banquet, Elda refuses to comply with the king's order to sing for him. Her dignity and defiance stand in sharp contrast to the pagan decadence and corruption of the court and harem of Belshazzar. Elda, who represents virtue and conviction, is a slave, but she and her people are superior in their faith and dignity. Neither promises nor threats can move her from the ways of virtue. She even tries to reason with the monarch on his responsibilities as king. Finally, she tells him that she is to be married to Rubén.

Before Belshazzar learns this, however, love transforms him. Everything is bathed in light ("Todo a mi vista se alumbra!") and his thoughts are ennobled ("Todo a mi mente se eleva!"). He yearns to forget that he is a king and to be just a man. Not knowing that Rubén is his rival for Elda, he frees him. In Act 3, however, he learns that Elda is promised to Rubén. A rebellious mob threatens the palace, and Rubén is dragged out to his death at the hands of the infuriated populace. In the final act of the play, the scene in which the prediction of doom appears on the palace wall during the great banquet, Elda reappears. She has gone mad, and, in her delirious pronouncements, also prophesies the destruction of Belshazzar's empire. In her insanity she relives her violation by the king and cries out to him to take pity on her innocence ("Ten piedad de mi inocencia!"). Even the corrupt ministers of the monarch feel compassion for her as she is carried away by slaves. The festivities briefly begin again, but the blind Joaquín condemns Belshazzar when he orders the sacred vessels of the temple of Jerusalem to be brought as drinking cups. Suddenly a great gust of wind blows open the windows and doors of the banquet room, thunder sounds, and the courtiers drop the sacred vessels to the floor. The words of doom appear written in fire on the wall, and Daniel enters to announce the coming victory of the Persians and the Medes. The Jews have been avenged, and will hear the voice of the Messiah. Belshazzar, who had gone out to meet the enemy, is brought back mortally wounded. His mother Nitocris sets fire to the palace, telling Daniel and Joaquín to flee.

The success of *Baltasar* was immediate and lasting, and newspaper reviews were uniform in their praise. The production was a sumptuous one, with the banquet scenes exploited for their rich possibilities of costume, music, and spectacle. The run was unprecedented for a serious play at that time, almost fifty consecutive performances before a brief closing to renovate costumes and scenery, followed by a reopening. Five days after the opening of *Baltasar*, however, tragedy struck la Avellaneda in the stabbing of her husband, Colonel Verdugo.

XVI *Two Final Lesser Works*

Two other plays written by la Avellaneda, *Catalina* and *El*

millonario y la maleta (*The Millionaire and the Suitcase*), were
not produced. The former, an adaptation of a play by Alexandre
Dumas and Auguste Maquet, was written in 1869. La Avellaneda
included it in the *Obras completas* of 1870. Like her other adaptations from the French, Tula altered the original story, modifying
the Roman conspirator Cataline and softening the violence of
the original. In her version, the conspiracy of Cataline and his
defeat are related to his personal life and his adulterous affair
with his mistress Fulvia.

The Millionaire and the Suitcase is a two-act farce recounting
the story of a mother with three marriageable daughters, Gabriela, Monica, and Rosa. Monica is clearly modeled on the pretentious young ladies of Moliere's *Précieuses Ridicules*. The mother,
doña Policarpa, learns that a millionaire bachelor, don Esteban,
is coming to visit his hometown, and prepares to capture him
for one of her daughters. A young man named Emilio, an attractive but poor artist, comes to town, and as his suitcase is also
initialed with an "E," is taken for the aging millionaire. The
farce, of course, depends on the mistaken identity. All ends well,
when don Esteban generously endows Emilio so that he can
marry the faithful and loving Gabriela.

The play, written for a group of amateurs in Seville, was not
performed. It is a light and charming satire that might have been
more fitting for the beginning of a career such as la Avellaneda's
rather than its ending. It was the last play, and one of the last
works that Tula wrote.

CHAPTER 4

The Novels

ALTHOUGH Spain, with *Don Quixote* and the development of the picaresque genre, has good reason to its claim as the "mother" of the novel, the rich vein of novelistic creativity had run dry long before the advent of romanticism to Iberia. By the 1830s and the advent of the romantic period, the works of Sir Walter Scott were widely read, often in poor translations, and there were numerous adaptations and versions of novels taken from the French. Spanish romantic writers devoted their energies primarily to poetry and to the drama, leaving a very slender list of novels. The two best known are Mariano José de Larra's *El doncel de don Enrique el doliente* (1834) and Enrique Gil y Carrasco's *El Señor de Bembibre* (1844). Both works belong to the medievalist traditions of the Scott type of novel, and are marked by a tone of melancholy and by descriptions of nature that link the works closely to the poetic writings of their authors.

The date of 1849 is usually given for the renaissance of the novel in Spain as a vital literary form, corresponding to publication of Fernán Caballero's *costumbristic* novel, *La gaviota* (*The Seagull*). Earlier, the scenes of Madrid life in the short writings of Mesonero Romanos, and later on, those sketches of Andalusian life by Estébanez Calderón, are usually cited as the forerunners of the realistic novel which would become the predominant literary form of the second half of the nineteenth century. Clearly, however, a fundamental change in the attitudes and outlook of Spanish society took place around 1840, with the establishment of the regency of General Espartero. Middle-class politics and middle-class tastes were rapidly becoming dominant. The period of romantic intensity that we usually ascribe to the triumph of *Don Alvaro o la fuerza del sino* in 1835 was rapidly modified.

In the early 1840s, as is visible in la Avellaneda's poetry and dramas, romantic excess was already on the wane. The ethical and aesthetic values of a vanished aristocracy could only be found in the remote Middle Ages, where writers such as Larra, Espronceda, and Gil y Carrasco sought the settings of their single historical novel. For la Avellaneda, conversely, the Medieval world was not a vehicle for prose drama. Tula utilized it in such plays as *Munio Alfonso* and *The Prince of Viana*, but even in her first theatrical venture, *Leoncia*, she was far closer to the bourgeois realistic drama than to the plays of her contemporary playwrights of the late 1830s. She was of her time, but was also ahead of it, as is also true of her novelistic production. Her romantic heroes and heroines find themselves more and more involved in a world of bourgeois materialism and implacable social mores, in short, a "prose world" rather than a poetic one. Even *Sab*, Tula's first novel, for all of its typically romantic figures and story, ends in a very real nineteenth-century world of commerce and burgeoning industry. Eclecticism is the keynote of Gertrudis's novels as also of her drama and her poetry. It has been a generally accepted critical position that la Avellaneda's novelistic production is inferior to her other work, an allegation by no means certain. This may explain why no serious study of her novels has ever been made. With the exception of *Sab*, none of the novels have been reprinted since the centennial edition of the complete works in 1914.[1] The same applies to the shorter prose works, the short stories, legends, and articles.

I *General Characteristics*

The novels do merit more extensive critical attention. Five of la Avellaneda's six works of sufficient length to be included in the category of novel clearly reflect broader developments in the European novel—the French novel in particular—of the middle decades of the century. Only one of the six, *Dolores*, is a historical novel set in the Middle Ages. In the prologue to *Dos mujeres* (*Two Women*), la Avellaneda pointedly informs the reader that the work reflects neither the descriptive historical genre ("género histórico descriptivo") of Walter Scott or the dramatic novel ("novela dramática") of Victor Hugo.[2] These two authors exercised great influence in Spain during these years but were not the only novelists being read. There were extensive publications of translations of other French authors whom Tula admired: Chateaubriand, Dumas père, George Sand, Lamartine, Rousseau, Bernardin de Saint Pierre, Scribe, Soulié, Madame de Staël, and Eugène Sue. The works of Fenimore Cooper reinforced the exoticism of Chateaubriand's vision of a vast and virgin America; Goethe's *Werther* ran through several editions. Tula makes no mention of him, but Balzac also was available in Spanish from 1836 on.[3] Perhaps la Avellaneda cannot be classed as a prolific or a great novelist, but she does show that novelistic production in Spain before the advent of the *costumbristic* novel was not confined exclusively to the stereotyped historical novel set in the Middle Ages.

If la Avellaneda avoids excessive neo-medievalism, she remains true to other fundamentally romantic tenets, themes, and characteristics already found in her poems and plays. Love is a constant and predominant motif, appearing as a natural and spontaneous passion, striking with all the force and suddenness of a bolt of lightning, affecting every aspect of the lover's life and feeling. It lifts the individual to the heights of ecstasy and plunges him or her into the depths of despair. Sublime and terrible, it transcends every other consideration, even morality, at least temporarily.

Love also has its price. Society sees to that, for the society reflected in the novels is every bit as mean-minded, petty and vindictive as in la Avellaneda's other writings. Social norm prevents private happiness, and the ideal and the real are in perpetual conflict. Heaven and earth are incompatible on the worldly plane; the capacity for feeling of Tula's heroes and heroines is far greater than their capacity to realize their hopes and their desires. Love's altar is stained with the blood of its victims. Illness, madness, suicide, and destruction follow in its wake, yet it is worth any sacrifice and any degree of suffering. Love's pain as well as love's delights surpass all other feelings. The virtuous are swept along with the culpable, but love is its own deity. Regardless of the disillusionment that it leaves behind, even its memory exalts. Tula's lovers never descend to the crass vulgarity of the Madame Bovaries of novelistic naturalism.

The settings for la Avellaneda's dramas of love vary from the exotic, natural, and picturesque scenes of her own native Cuba to the drawing rooms of Seville and Madrid, from the doomed Tenochtitlán of the latter-day Aztecs to the Rome and Naples of the Napoleonic era, and from fifteenth-century Spain to the eighteenth-century France of Louis XV and Madame de Pompadour. Only two novels are remote from Tulas's own era; the other four are, if not truly contemporary, at least fairly close in time to the author's own period. In this sense, Gertrudis was following in the footsteps of so-called romantics such as George Sand and Balzac who were already advancing the novelist's art toward realism.

Tula's poetry frequently relies on nature or some aspect of reality to embody or symbolize what she feels. In her novels, however, reality remains cruelly impassive for the most part. Death and suffering may destroy the individual, but society and the machinery of its functioning are indifferent, unaffected. No matter how noble the individual, no matter how great his capacity for love or for creativity, he cannot escape the reality that engulfs him. Sab dies a slave and Espatolino a bandit. Insight and inspiration ennoble the soul, but not the person. The lover perceives through love, but the rest of the world clings to its prejudices and its myopic monotony.

The themes and topics of the six full-length novels are wide ranging. In addition to romantic love, they include slavery in Cuba, the brutality of the Spanish conquistadors, landscapes running the gamut from the exoticism of the New World or the mountains of Italy to the mannered gardens of Versailles, costume and custom, vengeance, matrimony, and even the dangerous subject of divorce. Espatolino the bandit and Cuauhtemoc, the last Aztec emperor, are equally heroic in the tragedy and nobility of their defeat. Furthermore, in both *Espatolino* and her novel on the conquest of Mexico, Tula examines the question of power—of nations, of police, or of social classes—of justice, and of public and private morality. Much of what la Avellaneda expresses through Espatolino's words is close to the bitter pessimism of our own day in the postatomic world. Sab and Espatolino have been enslaved by social systems whose laws and justice have no room for compassion or virtue, that destroy the weak and exalt the strong. Poverty, illness, and death are present in all of the works, lending a serious and somber tone. The moments of happiness are short-lived, while violence and suffering are a vital part of all save one.

II *Type Figures*

The romantic stereotypes seen in Tula's dramas also appear in her novels, the most predominant being the romantic heroine, naive, trusting, total in her love for, and faith in, the man to whom she gives her heart, always vulnerable and susceptible in matters touching her emotions. She is the "good woman," physically beautiful but without overt sexuality, whose primary attractiveness is spiritual. Seemingly fragile, she can show great strength and tenacity. A good Catholic, capable of deep abnegation, she believes, and her faith sustains her. Prayer may be her only refuge in time of despair, or, like Dolores, she may enter a convent rather than compromise with the life of the world. She may have a rival who is, in some ways, a worthy adversary in the battle for the heart of a man. The Countess Catalina of *Two Women* or the Madame Pompadour of *The Boatman Artist* are talented and worldly ladies who are reputedly "bad women." Seemingly frivolous and sinful, they too are admirable: like the "good women," they are capable of deep love. Their superficial cosmopolitanism is only skin deep. The world has corrupted them, and they are doomed because of it, but fundamentally they retain the ability to long for the innocent paradise of Love's Garden of Eden. Even love, however, cannot triumph over the stricture of church and society.

The figure of the mother appears in several guises. As in the plays, a kindly and devoted nurse or servant may take on the maternal role. She may be no more than a saintly memory to be evoked with sighs and tears, as in *Sab* or in *The Boatman Artist*, or may appear as a long-suffering and pitiable figure, like Hubert Robert's mother in the latter novel. She may with equal frequency be an odious or even a monstrous character. Doña Leonor in *Two Women* does everything she can to smother the happiness and natural charm of her daughter. The mother of Dolores, for all of Tula's halfhearted attempts at modification of the character, matches Medea in her unnatural cruelty to her daughter and her heartless treatment of her husband.

The male characters in the novels range from the sensitive and self-sacrificing mulatto slave, Sab, to the heroic and defiant bandit, Espatolino, raised to the heights of the sublime through love, to the relatively prosaic Carlos, whose dilemma is love for two women, and the artistic and thoughtful Hubert Robert. Both Montezuma and Cuauhtemoc are doomed monarchs, the worthy adversaries of the ambitious but not wholly unsympathetic Hernán Cortez. The father figures of the novels are consistently kind and gentle parents, protective of the romantic heroines and trying, with one exception—Josefina's eccentric father in *The Boatman Artist*—to bring about the "good woman's" happiness. In *Sab*, there are two marked exceptions: both Carlota's beloved Carlos Otway and his father are materialistic and false, bent on exploiting the innocent heroine.

As in the lyrical poetry and in the plays, la Avellaneda herself is omnipresent behind various fictional roles throughout the novels. In three of the works, *Sab*, *Two Women*, and *The Boatman Artist*, the self-portrait is drawn through separate characters, representations of Tula's ego and alter ego: Carlota–Teresa, Luisa–Countess Carlota, and Josefina–Pompadour, respectively. The case of Dolores is even more curious, in that Tula insists in her prologue to the novel that she has invented nothing, yet proceeds to portray a young woman who historically did not exist but who has la Avellaneda's own baptismal name.

There are various secondary and minor characters, as might be expected, of differing interest and artistic success. Obviously, however, the talented but troubled Gertrudis continued her deep need to probe her own existence, in the novel as well as in the other forms that she cultivated. The phenomenon of her own life projected on a broad screen of fiction, the quest for identity, the unresolved search for absolutes, the struggles between flesh and spirit—the world of parties, honors, nobility, and the periodic withdrawals—the portraits of frustration and alienation, are what make the novels of continuing interest to us today.

Like Tula's other works, the novels partake of the excesses and flaws of the literature of the times. All too often, plot complications border on absurdity and the characters on caricature. Facile description replaces serious study or development of character. Descriptions frequently touch upon the grotesque or overly repugnant, while moments of beauty and happiness are excessive in their exaggeration. Tula is at her best in the novels, as in the plays, when writing in a realistic rather than a romantic vein. Then she is balanced and perceptive, with profound insights not only into the workings of the human heart and mind, but the growing materialism of the new society being formed in the middle years of the past century. The strong stand against slavery that *Sab* represents and the plea for individual dignity, and for justice for men and women, regardless of station or status, are concepts that have come into their own only in very recent years. In each of the novels, they are persistent and underlying themes. In this, as in so many other ways, la Avellaneda was before her time. The forms of novelistic expression which she used seem inadequate to us today, but the message is surprisingly modern. Tula's insights transcend the melodramatic extremes of her stories; her style and dialogue are frequently brilliant, as are many descriptive passages.

III Sab

La Avellaneda's first novel is, in a sense, her most interesting. It is abolitionist, with impassioned statements about slavery and the degradation of the individual which ring as true today as when Tula was writing them shortly after her arrival in Europe at age twenty-two. In one statement, the author affirms that she began the novel in Bordeaux. That was in 1836, and we suppose that she continued it while living with her stepfather's family in Galicia. Tula reveals in the prologue that she wrote the work in "momentos de ocio y melancolía" ("moments of idleness and melancholy"),[4] apparently as a means of passing the time in a period which was a difficult one for her. She also states that she had left it abandoned in a drawer for three years so, that, given the publication date of 1841, she would have finished the work in

1838. In a letter to don Antonio Neira dated February 1843, however, she writes that she began the work in Lisbon in 1838 and finished it in Seville in 1839 (SB, 15).

She mentions the work in two letters to Cepeda also. In one she notes that she has read ten chapters to a friend and in another she mentions the subscription money collected to underwrite the publication. At any rate, we know for certain that the book was written during the initial years of Tula's life in Spain, while the memories of her native Cuba were still vividly felt. It must have been written in part to soften her homesickness and to compensate for the disappointments encountered on the soil of her long-dead father.

Sab is a romantic novel given the marked importance of love and feeling of its main characters, but it is also part of the tradition of the Indianist novel, being set in the New World. For the European reader it would have appeared exotic, and follows in the traditions of the late eighteenth-century work of Bernardin de Saint Pierre's Paul et Virginie, which la Avellaneda knew and admired. The terrain and the flora and fauna of Cuba were sufficiently different from those of Spain that Tula frequently explains vocabulary via the use of footnotes in Sab. By the ending of the work, however, the romantic illusions of the principal characters have been destroyed. The only survivor, Carlota, must live in the real world of merchant, money and crass materialism, the world of realism rather than romanticism.

Sab, the protagonist for whom the novel is named, belongs to a long and illustrious line of romantic heroes, marked by destiny for frustration, suffering, and noble sacrifice. The best-known Spanish hero of this type is the duke of Rivas's don Alvaro who has survived down to our time as the protagonist in Verdi's opera La Forza del Destino. Sab is also a part of the family of such star-crossed lovers as Goethe's Werther and Chateaubriand's Chactas or René. All three figures had impressed Tula deeply, but Chateaubriand's influence is particularly noticeable. The story of Atala and Chactas, with its broad vistas and exotic landscapes of a virgin America, its wilderness highly colored and dramatized by what we would now call a "romantic style," parallel the landscapes of central Cuba in Sab. Chactas's love for the Christian Indian maiden, Atala, is as fatally impossible as is Sab's.

Furthermore, the mulatto slave is as melancholy and neurasthenic as René in his barely concealed and—barely controlled—
incestuous love for his sister. The burial scenes at the end of the
work also clearly recall the scenes of the missionary priest and
the grieving Chactas who place the body of Atala into a shallow
grave and set above it a crude and rustic wooden cross.

Sab's story is one of frustrated love. He is a mulatto slave
whose mother had been born a princess and free, but was brought
in slavery from the Congo. Life as a slave was unbearable for
her until she fell in love, but she would never reveal who Sab's
father was. Nevertheless, Sab did have a protector: it was none
other than don Luis de B——, uncle of the Carlota he adores and
brother of the present owner of the sugar mill plantation where
the family lives. Sab describes himself, saying that he belongs
"Pertenezco, —prosiguio con sonrisa amarga—, a aquella raza des-
venturada sin derechos de hombres.... soy mulato y esclavo."
("to that wretched race of men without rights.... I am a mulatto
and a slave."), (SB, 46). Consequently he is the first cousin of
Carlota, but also her personal slave. He wants to live and die in
her service, for he is the slave and captive of his love for her. That
love is without any hope of fulfillment on this earth, and Sab is
fully aware of this. He asks for no more than to serve Carlota, to
see her and to be near her if possible. His contemplation of her
is sheer bliss and the rapture of holding a lock of her hair
borders on madness. Consequently, his love is an unquenchable
thirst which thrives on its own torment, Wordsworth's "aching
joys" and "dizzy raptures" rather than the "dreary intercourse of
daily life."

Calota de B—— is nonetheless Sab's soul mate. She too is in
love's thrall. Her heart has been given to a young blond English-
man, Enrique Otway. Love fills her with joy when all goes well,
and with torment when obstacles seem to prevent their marriage. She loves fully, blindly, and spiritually, so much so that
even her cold and calculating fiancé is touched by the force and
nobility of her feeling. She is also another aspect of la Avellaneda
herself, the innocent and beautiful young Cuban girl, untouched
and untainted by the flesh or the practical realities of the world,
Eve without the apple tree. Indeed, Carlota seems to us today
rather like a sentimental schoolgirl, either too shortsighted or

too short-witted to see the reality before her eyes. Oblivious to the overpowering passion she has inspired in Sab, she remains equally blind to the cold calculations and mercenary interests of her husband-to-be and his money-grubbing father. She is, by today's standards, insipid, shallow, and, in her emotional myopia, inconsiderate of the needs and feelings of those around her. The adulation which everyone shows her is justifiable only in terms of her symbolic innocence.

Carlota de B——, however, was not created in our day, nor does she respond to our concepts of what constitutes an interesting, admirable, or intriguing young woman. In many ways, Carlota is a compendium of the heroine who briefly held center stage at the height of the Romantic age, and who even then was lampooned and satirized as an improbable simpleton. If we place her within the context that la Avellaneda creates for her, that of a cult of love which totally dominates the whole being and subordinates all else, her acts and her feelings become comprehensible. Tula professed her own ability to love in that way, a propensity which cost her dearly in her relationships with Cepeda and Tassara.

Consequently, Carlota must be seen as one of the innocent young romantic heroines, but she is also one of the many "goddesses" of love that people the pages of all of la Avellaneda's work. Her story does retain some individuality, and it is interesting to compare her to the two women in *Leoncia*, on which Tula was working at about the same time. She shares certain traits with both the adolescent Elena and the doomed and tortured Leoncia, but they are most alike in their total consecration to love, a fact that makes of them, as it does of Sab, superior beings. Carlota expresses this idea, albeit in moments of melancholy, when she recognizes that her beloved Enrique is not one of the superior beings: "... que hay almas superiores sobre la tierra, privilegiadas para el sentimiento y desconocidas de los almas vulgares; almas ricas de afectos, ricas de emociones ... para las cuales están reservadas las pasiones terribles, las grandes virtudes, los inmensos pesares ... y que el alma de Enrique no era una de ellas" ("... for there are superior souls on the earth, priviliged in matters of sentiment and unknown to vulgar souls; souls rich in affection, rich in emotions ... for whom the terrible passions, the highest virtues, and immense sorrows are reserved ... and the soul of Enrique is not one of them"), (*SB*, 74).

In another passage, she speaks of love and suffering, and asks if it is everyone's lot to feel so deeply: "¡Dios mío! ¿Se padece tanto siempre que se ama? ¿Aman y padecen del mismo modo todos los corazones. o has depositado en el mío un germen más fecundo de afectos y dolores? ... ¡Ah! si no es general esta terrible facultad de amor y padecer! ¡Cuán cruel privilegio me has concedido! ... porque es una desgracia, es una gran desgracia sentir de esta manera" ("Oh heavens! Does one always suffer so when one loves? Do all hearts love and suffer in the same way, or hast Thou placed in mine the most fertile seed of affection and of pain? ... Ah, if this terrible faculty of love and suffering is not a general thing, what a cruel privilege Thou hast given me! ... for it is an affliction, a great affliction to feel this way"), (*SB*, 74). This is, of course, Tula herself speaking through Carlota. We know that this concept of grandeur of soul was fundamental to her thinking. Sab expresses the same notion in a slightly different way. He and Enrique Otway leave the plantation just before the outbreak of a terrible storm, with Carlota entrusting her fiancé to the slave. When Otway is hit by a tree limb and knocked to the ground, Sab sees his opportunity to do away with his hated rival. He speaks of "un alma que supiera ser grande y virtuosa y que ahora puede ser criminal" ("a soul that knows how to be great and virtuous and that now could be criminal"), (*SB*, 76). Sab, of course, decides for virtue and nobility of action, and the dark horror of the storm gives way to splendid scenes of blue sky and celestial light.

Teresa, the poor and dependent cousin, is the third person endowed with this God-given faculty for love and spiritual superiority. She is Carlota's alter ego, the "dark sister" who is simultaneously another aspect of the fictional self-portrait of la Avellaneda in the novel. As she has no money, she has no status in the household, but serves as a sort of companion-servant to Carlota, obviously less than happy with her lot. She is consistently frowning and unsmiling. Sab is sufficiently insightful to recognize that she has deep feelings and even uncovers her mystery: she is in love with Enrique Otway herself. When Carlota, in her total insensitivity to her cousin, tells her that she loves Otway so much that even a word or a look means life or death to her heart, and then says that Teresa of course cannot understand this as she has never been in love, the latter replies quietly but surely: "Serás desgraciada si no moderas esa sensibilidad, pronta siempre a alarmarse" ("You will be very unhappy unless you moderate this sensitivity always so close to the danger point"), (*SB*, 146). Teresa moderates her own feelings. When Sab offers her the money which he won in the lottery, and which could buy Otway away from Carlota, Teresa realizes that such a maneuver would not really solve anything. She is too much of a realist for any scheme that would distort their own real intentions and feelings. At the end of the novel, Teresa has withdrawn from the world into a convent—a thing Tula repeatedly said she intended to do— and it is to her, until her death, that Carlota goes for consolation and guidance.

There is still another woman character who clings fiercely to her pride, but who, like Teresa, has no hope for the realization of her dreams: Martina. She is some sixty years old, and deeply marked by age and suffering. She too is a slave, and Sab is her adoptive son. Her grandson Luis is a pathetic and grotesquely deformed little boy who clings to Sab. Martina's physical ugliness, however, conceals a noble soul capable of deep devotion. She thinks of herself as a princess of the Indian race that the Spaniards destroyed, and she is portrayed as a wise woman who knows medicine and the lore of the past of her vanished people. As she lives near Cubitas, an area near Puerto Príncipe where Tula grew up, it is possible that she is in fact a portrait of someone whom Gertrudis actually knew. Certainly the descriptions of the outing to her village are based on trips taken there during Tula's childhood and adolescence.

IV *Antislavery Sentiment*

The theme of slavery is one that is reiterated again and again. Given that fact, it is difficult to understand why some critics have seen the theme of slavery as peripheral or as an unimportant detail. Cotarelo y Mori, whose book on la Avellaneda is by far the most extensive study yet made, makes a very curious statement. Noting that some writers have wanted to see in *Sab* an abolitionist novel similar to *Uncle Tom's Cabin*, he remarks: "No hay nada de protesta contra la esclavitud, más que el hecho de admitir en el héroe el impedimento de aspirar a su dicha" ("there is nothing of protest against slavery, except for the fact of admitting in the hero the obstacle to his happiness").[5] He quotes Nicomedes Pastor Díaz to the effect that Sab could have been anyone else, in any other society, and still have had the same problem. Tula did not place the action in another setting or another society, however. She placed it in the Cuba in which she had grown up, in the very town and countryside in which she had grown up, and in which several acute problems in the controversy over slavery had come to a head. She and her family were fully aware of the many aspects, moral and economic, of the slavery question. We can assume from *Sab* that her family were also slave owners. In 1822, there was unrest, and in 1826, the attempted insurrection of Frasquito came to an end with the execution of the leaders in Puerto Príncipe. An 1827 census of the Island gave the following statistics: 311,051 whites, 286,942 Negro slaves, and 106,494 freed blacks.[6] Tula obviously knew exactly what she was doing and saying when she wrote *Sab*.

There is no doubt that the subject was singularly controversial and even inflammatory. For the daughter of a highly placed military family to have written the unmistakable attack against slavery that she did, must have created much tension within the family. Understandably, she did not include it in the *Obras Completas* as she designed them before her death. It is commendable that the work was reinstated in the edition of 1914.

Carmen Bravo Villasante, in her recent edition of *Sab*, gives a much sounder critical opinion on the matter of slavery in the novel (*SB*, 20–24). She is right when she says that Sab belongs to the series of romantic outcasts from society—the pirate, bandit, and beggar—but at the same time Sab reminds the reader that he is exiled from humanity because of his color as well as his condition of slavery. This makes the contrast to the blond Anglo-Saxon, Enrique Otway, all the more striking and the point of color of the skin all the more significant. La Avellaneda is concerned with racism as well as the institution of slavery, but it is to the inhuman cruelties of the latter that she addresses passage after passage, placed primarily in the mouth of Sab.

The theme appears in the very first pages of the book, in the initial encounter between the unknown arrival—Enrique Otway—and the mysterious "native" of the area, Sab. The stranger, seeking his way to Bellavista, the sugar-mill plantation of don Carlos de B——, encounters Sab, and the two begin to talk. Otway asks about the plantation, and Sab replies that things are not going well. Times are bad; there are only fifty slaves left. Otway's comment is significant: "Vida muy fatigosa deben tener los esclavos en estas fincas,... y no me admira que se disminuya considerablemente su número" ("The slaves on these country estates must have a very harsh life,... and I'm not surprised that their number is greatly reduced"), (*SB*, 44). Sab's lengthy reply embodies the attitude which Tula reiterates throughout the work:

"Es un vida terrible a la verdad," respondió el labrador arrojando a su interlocutor una mirada de simpatía: "bajo este cielo de fuego el esclavo casi desnudo trabaja toda la mañana sin descanso, y a la hora terrible de mediodía, jadeando, abrumado bajo el peso de la leña y de la caña que conduce sobre sus espaldas, y abrasado por los rayos del sol que tuesta su cutis, llega el infeliz a gozar todos los placeres que tiene para la vida; dos horas de sueño y una escasa ración.... ¡Ah! sí, es el cruel espectáculo la vista de la humanidad degradada, de hombres convertidos en brutos, que llevan en la frente la marca de la esclavitud y en su alma la desperación del infierno."

"It is a terrible life indeed," answered the countryman with a friendly look at his interlocutor: "underneath this sky of flame, the half-naked slave works the day through without rest, and at the hour of the terrible midday, panting, crushed under the weight of the firewood and of the sugar cane that he carries on his shoulders, and burned by the rays of the sun that roasts his skin, the poor soul finally tastes of the only pleasure that he has in all of his life: two hours of sleep and a meager ration.... Ah yes, it is a cruel spectacle, this scene of degraded humanity, of men turned into brutes, who carry on their brows the mark of slavery and in their soul the desperation of hell."   (*SB*, 44–45)

At this point Sab reveals to Otway who he is; that he is a part of that unhappy race that have no rights, a slave and a mulatto. Otway changes his tone of address immediately, speaking down to the man whom up till then he had addressed as an equal. Otway's father openly insults Sab, who is but an inferior being after all!

In other passages, Sab is no less vehement in his expression. He has no family, no life. He is a man without a country ("los esclavos no tienen patria"), for a slave is no more than a beast of burden ("los deberes del esclavo son deberes de la bestia de carga"), (*SB*, 168). Sab's most vehement indictment comes in the letter he writes just before his death to Teresa, asking how she, who is only a weak woman, could show more strength than he, a man. He questions if it is virtue, and then asks of himself, "just what is virtue?" No man has satisfied his quest for a comprehension of it. Even the church supports slavery and the debasement of human beings: "Me acuerdo que cuando mi amo me enviaba a confesar mis culpas a los pies de un sacerdote, yo preguntaba al ministro de Dios qúe haría para alcanzar la virtud, 'La virtud del esclavo—se respondía, es obedecer y callar, servir con humildad y resignación a sus legítimos dueños, y no juzgarlos nunca'" ("I remember," he writes, "that when my master sent me to confess my sins at the feet of a priest, I asked the minister of God what I should do to attain virtue. 'The virtue of the slave,' he answered, 'is to obey and keep silent, to serve with humility and resignation his legitimate owners, and never to judge them'"), (*SB*, 220).

Sab then goes on to examine various facets of life and justice, fundamental matters in all of the work of la Avellaneda in varying degree, as we know. He questions why some have the right to enslave and others the obligation to obey, how God who has written equality on every tombstone could condemn a slave to forget the very dignity that has been given to him through his birth as a human being. Sab has searched in vain for virtue among men: "He visto siempre que el fuerte oprimía al débil, que el sabio enganaba al ignorante, y que el rico despreciaba al pobre. No he podido encontrar entre los hombres la gran armonía que Dios ha establecido en la naturaleza" ("The strong oppress the weak, the wise deceive the ignorant, and the rich scorn the poor. I have been unable to find among men the great harmony that God has established in nature"), (*SB*, 221). Sab asks if he is to blame if God has given him a soul and a heart, and the ability to love beauty, justice, and greatness. He questions why he must suffer the terrible struggle between his true nature and his bitter destiny. He finally concludes that it is not God, but men who "have formed this destiny," that it is they who have cut the wings that God gave to his soul. It is not only the slave who suffers. Women also suffer, for they too are the victims of society's laws: "¡Pobres y ciegas víctimas! Como los esclavos, ellas arrastran pacientemente su cadena y bajan la cabeza bajo el yugo de las leyes humanas" ("Poor and blind victims! Like slaves they patiently drag their chain and lower their heads beneath the yoke of human laws. With no other guide but an ignorant and credulous heart, they choose a master for their whole life"), (SB, 227). Woman's slavery is marriage, from which she has no recourse on this earth. The slave can change masters or hope to gather together enough money to buy his liberty, but woman "pero la mujer, cuando levanta sus manos enflaquecidas y su frente ultrajada para pedir libertad, oye el monstruo de voz sepulcral que la grita: 'En la tumba'" ("when she lifts her emaciated hands and her abused forehead to ask for freedom, hears the monster with the voice from the grave that cries out: 'In the tomb'"), (SB, 227).

Sab talks of death, as does Teresa. They see it as a release from suffering, and death comes to Martina, to Luis, and to the faithful dog Leal by the end of the book. Carlota has married her beloved Enrique Otway, but soon realizes her error. Her life, to be lived out in the knowledge of the superior love of Sab for her and among the materialistic and heartless people who make up the world of her husband's business associates, is a kind of death. The moment of her marriage and the supposed beginning of her great happiness is also the very moment of Sab's death. "Tales contrastes los vemos cada día en el mundo: ¡Placer y dolor!" ("Such contrasts we see every day in this world: Pleasure and pain!"), (SB, 221), writes la Avellaneda. Five years later, the romantic heroine is a tearful and unhappy middle-class wife, suffocated in a mercantile and speculative atmosphere that has destroyed all of her youthful illusions. She has come to know the source of the comfort and luxury in which she had lived and which she had once taken for granted. She sees her husband for what he is and, Tula tells us, begins to comprehend

Life. Her dreams have been dissipated, her love and her happiness have disappeared; romanticism has given way to realism. Tula recognizes that the illusions of romanticism are a deception that cannot withstand the assault of logic or contact with the real world for very long. Carlota and Sab are both romantic figures, but they love and live in the material world from which, ultimately, there is escape only through dreams, through madness, or through death, precisely the solutions that la Avellaneda has recourse to in her dramas and other prose works.

V Dos mujeres

Just as *Sab* offers a picture of life and nature in central Cuba during the time la Avellaneda was growing up there, so *Dos mujeres* (*Two Women*) portrays the Seville and Madrid of the late 1830s and early 1840s when Tula was living in those two cities. She had gone to Seville in 1838 and taken up residence there with her brother Manuel; later her mother had joined them with her three younger children. There Tula began her literary career and there she met the maleficent Cepeda, refused the hand of Mendez Vigo, and started tongues wagging about her indecorous behavior. In 1840, her hopes of marriage to Cepeda for the time at an end, she moved to Madrid, stepping onto the national, and even international, stage of the artistic world. With the publication of her *Poesías* and *Sab* in 1841, she became established professionally and socially. As we know, however, she was not really happy, and her second novel provides a fictional chronicle of Tula's early years in Spain, first in Seville and then in Madrid.

The story which is her vehicle—and which is familiar from the dramas—is a tale of frustrated love. Two women, to a degree the Carlota and Teresa of *Sab* reworked, love the same young man, Carlos de Silva, a love triangle involving three characters of clearly romantic mold, but living very much in the prosaic society in which Carlota ended her days. The realistic ambience is far removed from the romantic fictions which Scott or Victor Hugo set in exotic places or medieval times, a fact which Tula herself underlines in the prologue written for the novel's publication in 1842. She declares that she is not writing to fit into any set genre, but trying to achieve verismilitude in this novel (i.e., she is not consciously following any doctrine of realism), but as we shall see, she does write in a manner which less than a decade later will begin to take shape as the realistic novel. The use of specific names, places, dates, and the detailed descriptions of costume and custom, domestic and social life in nineteenth-century Seville and Madrid, are all techniques normally ascribed to the novel of the second half of the century, not to 1842.

The actual time in which Tula sets the work is 1817. There seems to be no specific reason for that particular date, except that this places the action after the end of the Napoleonic wars, but does not require descriptions of the industrial and commercial changes such as those reflected in the final passages of *Sab*. It also conceivably justified in the author's mind the repressive remarks made by doña Leonor in the opening pages of the work. The reign of Ferdinand VII had been over only three years when la Avellaneda came to Spain, and she was surely aware that only when that tyrannical and bigoted monarch died did romanticism and moderate liberalism finally come to Spain.

In the work, Don Francisco de Silva is a widower with a young and handsome son, Carlos, who has been studying in Paris. His widowed sister, doña Leonor, has a beautiful and demure young daughter, Luisa. Carlos and Luisa, first cousins, were very close in childhood, but have not seen each other in eight years. Doña Leonor, who acted as a foster mother to her nephew, sees in him a good and suitable match for her daughter. She rails at her brother for sending his son to study in Paris, that Ninevah of corruption and heresy, and has a fainting spell when she hears that don Francisco intends to send Carlos temporarily to Madrid when he returns to Spain. The brother yields to his sister's emotional blackmail, agreeing that Carlos should come home to Seville to stay, and, presumably, to wed the bride decided on for him.

The domestic life of doña Leonor's comfortable home is described for us in detail, emphasizing the cramped and stuffy atmosphere of a well-to-do but narrowly provincial family held in tight control by the fastidious and pious mother. If doña Leonor is—as we may reasonably suppose—a portrait of doña Francisca de Arteaga, Tula's own mother (she uses the masculine form of the name, Francisco, for the henpecked brother) it is hardly complimentary. The portrait, in fact, borders on satire. Doña Leonor is wholly inflexible in her living and her thinking. Tula writes of her that she could have been moved back into the seventeenth century, that is to say, long before the period of the Enlightenment, without any change in either her house or her family. Her only company consists of two aging ladies who are as devout and devoted to churchgoing as she, her venerable confessor, and two doddering gentlemen who still talk of the wedding of Charles IV to María Luisa more than half a century earlier. Every Saturday, she goes to confession, and every Sunday she attends mass. Luisa is held in total submission to her mother.

Tula carefully describes Luisa's education, primarily religious, including no music or dance, but a lot about household matters, embroidery and sewing, the rudiments of mathematics and geography, and the forced memorization of some sacred history. She was allowed reading of the lives of the saints and of Fray Luis, had no friends of her own age, and went out only with the aged friends of her mother. What "naughty" reading she did was of novels smuggled to her by her doting uncle, such works as *Paul et Virginie* (one of Tula's favorites). It is an education that la Avellaneda obviously found very wanting, and through her description of it and her tying it to a mother who lamented the ending of the Holy Inquisition, she clearly means it as criticism of the faulty education of women in her time.

At seventeen, there was nothing about Luisa to lead one to believe that she had "una de aquellas almas de fuego, una de aquellas imaginaciones poderosas y activas que se devoran a sí mismas si carecen de otro alimento" ("one of those souls of fire, one of those powerful and active imaginations that devour themselves if they do not have other sustenance"), (*OB* V, 15). She is an angelic creature, painted almost like a Murillo madonna: "La inocencia brillaba en cada una de sus facciones como en cada uno de sus pensamientos, y cuando sus ojos azules y serenos se levantaban a lo alto, y un rayo de luz argentaba su blanca frente, diríase que recordaba en la tierra la existencia del Cielo" ("Innocence shone in every one of her features as in every one of her thoughts, and when her blue and untroubled eyes looked upward, and a ray of light lit up her white forehead,

you would think that she was recalling here on earth the
existence of Heaven"), (*OB* V, 15). This lovely Eve finds her
Adam in her cousin, Carlos, when the two see each other at a
carefully arranged get-together at doña Leonor's, surrounded by
the usual cronies. Youth speaks to youth, and the cousins quickly
recognize their love. Their marriage takes place.

While their personal happiness transcends the dismal domestic
atmosphere of doña Leonor's home where they continue to live,
their circumstances are presented in terms both of romantic love
and realistic daily life. This would, of course, end the story without much drama were la Avellaneda not to introduce some plot
reversal. Carlos must go to Madrid to tend to a family inheritance,
meeting temptation in the form of the Countess Catalina de S.
The peace and monotony to which Carlos had longed so to
return is soon gone, never to be recovered. Luisa lives on in her
idyll, the absence of her husband making all of life around her
seem empty. She trusts completely.

The Madrid that la Avellaneda draws for us is one that she
knew intimately, the world of smart society, of dinner parties,
brittle and often cynical conversation, gossip and backbiting, all
carried out in sumptuous settings of opulence and wealth. It is
also the world of the theater boxes where men and women of
a glittering but superficial social group exhibit their clothes,
jewels, and conquests. Carlos's cousin Elvira, with whom he
stays in Madrid, lives on the fringes of this society, but Catalina
is at its very center when Carlos first meets her. If Luisa embodies the Tula of years past, Catalina is the self-portrait, in
many ways, of the Gertrudis who entered the Madrid literary
and social world with such stunning impact in 1840, as becomes
apparent in the conversation at the first dinner party to which
Carlos goes. The Countess Catalina soon becomes the main topic
of conversation, and one of the male guests sings her praises,
calling her "distinguished" because of her brilliant talents, her
fine education, and her elegance. He finishes his comments by
saying that he feels this way in spite of the things said about
her by jealous rivals, which produces a spate of protests. How
could anyone be envious of such a flirt? Finally, a blond young
man, the lover of one of the older women at the table declares:
"yo detesto a esas *mujeres hombres* que de todo hablan, que de

todo entienden, que de nadie necesitan..." ("I detest those mannish women who can talk on any subject, understand everything, and have need of no one..."), (*OB*, V, 51). The identification of this remark with Tula is unmistakable. By this time, the oft-repeated comment that was attributed to Breton de los Herreros, had been made: "Es mucho hombre esta mujer" ("That woman is a lot of man"); and, as Tula was to write in her autobiography of 1850, she was already the target of slander and noxious remarks.

The malicious attacks continue during the dinner party, as one woman questions how the countess could survive without her surrounding cult of adorers. A married woman who lost her husband's affections to the charms of the countess seemingly rises to the latter's defense. The countess, she says, is the finest singer in Madrid, a talented dancer and artist, and a woman who is so well educated that she can talk on their level with the most knowledgeable men on morals, religion, and politics. She concludes by saying there is no other woman in Spain of such liberal opinions. Carlos is sufficiently embarrassed by the reputation of Catalina to deny any family relationship with her. He has no wish to meet the countess, but his cousin Elvira insists that he accompany her to a ball. There was one at her friend's home every week, to which the most brilliant of Madrid's society came. The countess's mansion is beautiful, with everything in excellent taste. The finest of society and the elegant simplicity of the setting are described as worthy of the most distinguished gatherings of Paris. When Elvira presents Carlos to Catalina, there is a moment of confusion. Carlos blushes, and this slight timidity makes him particularly appealing.

The countess, described at length, is thin, with lovely shoulders and neck, graceful in her bearing, but her major charm is in the expressiveness of her face and the brilliance of her look. She is aristocratic and dignified, but comfortably relaxed. Carlos examines her from head to toe, and after his beloved Luisa, finds her strikingly seductive. He avoids, however, the author tells us, the profanation of comparing the lovely and elegant figure before him with the celestial image in his heart.

Not until the second meeting does Carlos begin to see the falsity of the portrait of the countess that had been painted at the dinner party. There is nothing pretentious about her conversation, which, on the contrary, charms him. The mutual attraction has begun, and continues on the third meeting at the theater. Seated in the countess's box, Carlos tells her of his love for Luisa, and Catalina tells him, in the same terms as those of Sab or of Carlota, that only a superior heart could feel such love. She asks if Lusia is worthy of such feeling. It is then that Carlos replies that *his wife* is an angel, and Catalina, stricken, learns that the man to whom she is attracted has been married for almost a year.

Elvira's illness brings Carlos and Catalina together again, and Carlos' admiration grows. Their conversation—written in excellent dialogue by la Avellaneda—covers many subjects: society, happiness, love, and marriage. Catalina recounts her earlier life with her late husband in the Paris of the First Empire. But she has not been happy, nor has she ever truly loved: "Felices aquellos a quienes cupo el destino de amar y ser amados, y ¡felices también los que no sienten la estéril y devorante necesidad de una ventura que les fue rehusada!" ("Happy are those whose destiny it is to love and be loved, and happy as well those who do not feel the sterile and devouring necessity for a happiness that has been denied them"), (*OB*, 79). Catalina has filled the void in her soul with activities: "También hay opio para el corazón y para el espírtu; y ese opio es la disipacíon" ("There is an opium for the heart and for the spirit also; and that opium is dissipation"), (*OB*, 81). Her statements concerning what women look for in a man constitute a compelling image of what Tula herself sought, but did not find: heart, admiration that is not overcoming, domination that does not tyrannize, the ability to love and to appreciate the man who lifts through his own superiority without humiliating. Further on, Catalina declares that a woman will always forgive a lack of intelligence in a man sooner than a lack of feeling. The novelist is obviously criticizing Cepeda in these passages, as some of the same things were said in the love letters to him.

The life of Catalina's youth provides a picture of the Paris that Balzac was immortalizing at the same time Tula was writing *Two Women*. The husband she describes, the aristocratic roué of the Old Regime, worn out by love and genteel excesses, will reappear in her portrait of Louis XV in *The Boatman Artist*. Catalina read Rousseau's *Julie* and Goethe's *Werther*, and while living in the marriage arranged for her at sixteen by her mother, felt as she read the novels "páginas de fuego que me presentaba su mano fría . . ." ("pages of fire that held out their cold hand to me . . ."), (*OB*, 81). She speaks of her youthful love fantasies and of her idealization of the men she was attracted to. She was also cruelly deceived, at which point she turned to more serious reading, to a study of intelligence and sensitivity in the works of Plato and Rousseau. The problems of social life, with its hypocrisy and temptations, had fascinated her. She comprehends the glory of men's exploits as politicians or soldiers and asks what is left to a woman. The fundamental problem that she presents, however, is one of identity, of the individual in the context of his private life, and in that of his social and public life.

Both Carlos and Catalina struggle in vain against the love that soon overwhelms and possesses them. Even Carlos's "pure" love for Luisa is insufficient to defend him. Nevertheless, the two decide that they must part. Carlos takes a coach to return to Seville to his home and wife, but by this time, he is a changed person. His love for Catalina has brought him a knowledge of the world that he had not conceived of before. The countess has shown him his ignorance. In the coach that Carlos takes, there is a second passenger, so wrapped in her cape that he cannot see her face. At a stop to change horses, the woman awakens. It is Catalina. Destiny that brought them together in the first place has brought them together again, and Carlos returns to Madrid with his loved one. Catalina tells him that although people say that adultery is a crime, there is no adultery for the heart. There is, nonetheless, adultery for Luisa and for Carlos's father who comes to Madrid when the wayward husband does not return. Luisa learns of the love affair and finally goes to the countess's country home and there confronts her. The scene, highly dramatic, is reminiscent of similar confrontations in Tula's stage plays. Catalina, with great nobility of soul, decides to give Carlos up to his legitimate wife, and is shortly thereafter found a suicide by asphyxiation by her friend Elvira, who is unable to resuscitate her.

The final chapter of the novel, the kind of epilogue that also ends *Sab*, takes place in 1826, seven years after Catalina's death. Carlos has returned from his post in London and goes to the grave of the woman whom he loved and who had died in her twenty-fifth year. Back at his home in Madrid, friends come to call. Two men on leaving the house discuss Carlos's life. He has risen to high diplomatic importance, but he is very seldom at home. There are rumors that he was deeply saddened by the loss of a loved one, and that since her death, he is all ambition. The two men pass a lady on the street. It is Elvira with her two daughters. The elder has dark, burning eyes, and her name is Catalina. Elvira visits Carlos and Luisa, and en route home tells her daughters that Luisa is a very good woman, but a very unhappy one. When the daughters are older, she says, she will relate to them the story of "two women."

It is the voice of la Avellaneda that speaks in the last paragraphs, pondering whether the truth can make any difference, if the story of Luisa and Catalina can reveal anything of worth to these two young girls—anything more than the fact that woman's lot is unhappiness. The impossibility of dissolving the bonds of matrimony converts them into chains by which women are destroyed. The world is indifferent to them and to their suffering, but is quick to notice any indiscretion and to condemn. The implacable hangman is there whether the individual woman is virtuous or not.

The interest of *Two Women* goes beyond the work as a novel. It is an insightful and penetrating psychological and social document. Like *Sab*, it tells the fictional story of star-crossed lovers in the romantic tradition. They live, however, in a real world from which they cannot escape and which dooms the realization of their emotions and aspirations. By the time of writing of this second novel, Tula has mastered the mechanics of plot and dialogue, and when we consider the date of publication of 1842, we more clearly realize the author's incisive social conscience that put her well ahead of her time and contributed to her profound sense of alienation. What makes it all the more impressive is Tula's age: she was twenty-eight years old, and just on the threshold of her career.

VI Espatolino

La Avellaneda's third full-length novel is based on the life story of the Italian bandit, Spatolino, whose name Tula uses in the Hispanized form, Espatolino. The novel was first published in serial format in *El Laberinto* in Madrid. Publication began on January 1, 1844, and concluded in August of the same year. The work was republished in a single volume two years later in 1858.

The historical figure whose story Tula recounts in *Espatolino* was shot in Rome in 1807, a notorious bandit chief who had robbed and plundered for a period of eighteen years, stopping coaches, kidnapping passengers, and even murdering them. The area from Rome to Naples was under his power, and it was only by a trick that the French governor—Napoleon had placed Murat on the throne of the Kingdom of Two Sicilies in the period during which the events took place—was able to bring Espatolino to justice. The strategem was to offer the bandit a pardon on condition that he betray his own men. Espatolino agreed, and he, his wife, and eight of his men were taken prisoner and put on trial.

The trial lasted five months. There were some four hundred witnesses. Espatolino tried to save his wife and four of his men. The other four he considered traitors. Among the police officers assigned to guard Espatolino there was one who had been a part of his band, years before. He was recognized by some of the witnesses and brought to trial for participation in a murder. Espatolino himself displayed a ferocity and courage during the trial that made his legend all the more spectacular. He even lamented those occasions for committing crimes that he had missed. Finally, Espatolino, four companions, and the police officer were condemned to death. Espatolino's wife was sentenced to four years in prison. The bandit chief himself refused to confess and laughed at his companions who did talk with the priest sent to comfort them before their deaths. Before the firing squad, he not only refused to have his eyes covered, but actually gave the order to fire. After his death, several plays and a biography were written about him.[7]

Apparently there were readers of the first two chapters of

Tula's novel who thought that the work was a translation from the Italian. With the publication of the third installment in *El Laberinto*, the author included a statement telling her readers that the work was an original one and not a translation. She also gave the source for her basic story as an article which had appeared in a foreign newspaper about the imprisonment and trial of Espatolino. The article had been translated and reprinted in Havana, where Tula had read it. She says that the article contained only a brief résumé of the trial, and consequently the rest of her story is one that she invented, as she did not know any other works about the bandit chief. Nevertheless, Tula did know enough of the true history to utilize the real name of the police officer, Angelo Sotoli, who brought about the arrest. She also did sufficient research to give a credible description of the Italian countryside, despite the fact that she had never personally been to Italy.

Tula does indeed write a story of her own invention. Central to it is the love of Espatolino and his wife Anunciata, the niece of an Italian agent of the French police whom Espatolino had seduced and carried off to become his wife. She does not know the identity of her husband, who has taken a false name, Giuliano, and so it is love that gives identity to the person. When Anunciata asks about his position in the world, Espatolino replies: "Mi posición en el mundo! ¿Qué te importa, si es verdad que me amas?" ("My position in the world! What difference does it make to you if it is true that you love me?"), (*OB* V, 220). Further on he asks: "Si el destino hiciese de tu amante un ser desventurado y aborrecido del mundo, ¿no se mudaría tu corazón?" ("If destiny were to make of your lover an unfortunate being who is hated by the world, wouldn't your heart change?"), (*OB* V, 203). Anunciata replies with an energetic "Never," and says that she would demand to be a part of whatever good or bad luck should be her husband's lot.

Anunciata's role is essentially a repetition of that of Carlota in *Sab* and of Luisa in *Two Women*. She is the all-believing, all-trusting romantic heroine who is without guile or subterfuge. Her idealism is shattered, however, for it is she who naively persuades Espatolino to accept the pardon of the police official, and consequently, it is she who seals her lover's doom. When she realizes that she has brought about Espatolino's death through her blind and undiscerning trust in the villainous Rotoli, she becomes insane, another of la Avellaneda's angelic females who is destroyed by contact with the real world.

Espatolino is in many ways the romantic hero, but there is also much that belongs to the picaresque tradition in his story. Tula makes of him an Italian Robin Hood, clearly utilizing him to express her own ideas on power and justice. She glorifies him, affirming that one has but to mention his name in Italy to hear his exploits praised by the poets, and that women will recount the stories of "el ingenio y el crimen, la ferocidad y el heroísmo" ("his talent and crime, ferocity and heroism"), (*OB* V, 258). He is a man with the mission of avenging the weak and oppressed ("poseía la terrible misión del vengador de los débiles y de los oprimidos"), (*OB* V, 258).

His own life has made him cynical and bitter in all things except his love for Anunciata and his memories of his mother. His tale is one of injured innocence and trust. He had deeply believed in honor, in hard work and honesty. His best friend was Count Carlos, and his youthful beloved was an orphan girl named Luigia. His father's trusted friend, Sarti, betrays the father's confidence, bringing about his bankrupcy. He even seduces and marries Luigia, but Espatolino still has confidence in his friend Carlos. When the latter falls ill with the plague, only Espatolino has the courage to care for him, and subsequently, almost dies of the illness himself. Once both are recovered, Count Carlos seduces Espatolino's sister, gets her pregnant, and then abandons her. When she dies, shamed and shunned by all but her ruined family, the pitiful funeral procession is forced to make way for the baptismal procession of the count's first-born legitimate child. His mother dies of illness and worry and is turned over to a medical group to be dissected for anatomical studies. The father dies in prison. Espatolino himself challenges the count to a duel, and is put into prison. It is then that he becomes a bandit, making war on all of society, and finally has his personal revenge; he captures Sarti and literally makes him eat his own gold; he turns the wife of Count Carlos over to his men to be raped and then returns her to her husband.

Espatolino's declarations on the prison system, on justice,

and on power make him the spiritual brother of Sab in his attack on slavery. He sees that prisons are the schools of crime: "Allí crece, en corrompida atmósfera, la contagiosa lepra del crimen, y por eso aunque entran muchos con sentimientos de hombre, ninguno sale sin instintos de fiera" ("It is there that the contagious leprosy, in a corrupted atmosphere, grows, and for that reason, although many enter with the feelings of men, not one comes out without having the instincts of a wild beast"), (OB V, 249). Espatolino cries out that justice is an empty word and a repugnant sarcasm, for only force is justice in this world. Right is on the side of those who triumph. Napoleon, he declares, raised his throne on mountains of dead bodies. Only one law is valid for Espatolino, and it is that of necessity. He justifies his life as a bandit, saying that he makes war on men just as they make war between themselves. There is a difference, however, for Espatolino is consciously and openly dishonest: "ellos matan con las calumnias, con las difamaciones, con las perfidias, y yo con el hierro, que hace menos larga la agonía: ellos roban con disfraces, y yo presento francamente el rostro del bandido" ("men kill with slander, with vilification, with perfidy, and I with steel, which makes the agony shorter; they rob with disguises, and I present my bandit's face openly"), (OB V, 267).

Neither the crown nor the church are spared his attack. Where Sab was told by the priest that full submission was his only lot, Espatolino says that the church condones condemning the criminal to death even though he is repentent. One day, however, the death penalty will be done away with: "no dudemos... de que llegará un día en que ella, la misericordia, ilumine la mente de los legisladores de la tierra, haciendo desaparecer la horrenda venganza social que llaman pena de muerte" ("let us not doubt... that the day will come when compassion will illuminate the minds of the legislators of the earth, causing the horrible social revenge that we call the pain of death to disappear"), (OB V 249). He compares the crown of the monarch and the tiara of the pope to the dagger in his hand, affirming that they are one and the same: "instrumentos de diferentes formas destinados al mismo fin... armas para la lucha en que cada egoísmo se esfuerza para entronizarse" ("instruments of different forms, destined to the same end... arms for the struggle in which each ego strives to enthrone itself"), (OB V, 249).

Espatolino's own end exemplifies his point of view. He is a victim of his trust in his wife, who naively begs him to turn himself over to the authorities. At first he is too noble to do so because of the condition that he also turn in his own companions. Once they betray him, however, he decides to follow Anunciata's fervent pleas, stating that even if his hands are cut off, or he is blinded, so long as he can hear Anunciata's voice he will accept what punishment is meted out to him. He learns too late, however, that both he and Anunciata have been fooled. Anunciata has sold her husband into the hands of the hangman. The horror of this is too much for her to bear: she goes mad, and Espatolino goes to his death.

VII Guatimozín, último emperador de México

For her fourth full-length novel, la Avellaneda returned to a subject and a figure that had fascinated her already in her adolescence: Hernando Cortez (Hernán Cortés). She had written a play (now lost) about him and his conquest of Mexico. In the novel she again takes up his story, but gives the novel the title of Montezuma's successor *Guatimozín, último emperador de México (Cuauhtemoc, The Last Aztec Emperor)*. It was published both in serial form—it began in *El Heraldo* of Madrid on February 20, 1846—and as a single volume, also in 1846. In Mexico there was a second printing in 1853 and a third printing in 1887. In 1898, an English translation appeared, also in Mexico, done by one Helen Edith Blake, who says that la Avellaneda's dramas were "still standard in Spain" (i.e., in 1898). Her prologue states that Tula's novels have fallen into neglect, and that only two copies of *Cuauhtemoc* could be found in Mexico City as the book "is entirely out of print, although among literary Spanish-Americans it is considered equal, if not superior, to Lew Wallace's 'Fair God,' which covers the same epoch and historical events and resembles it in many respects." Mrs. Blake then speaks of the charge of plagiarism that had been leveled against Wallace: "in fact, it has been freely charged that the 'Fair God' is a plagiarism of *Cuauhtemoc*, but a perusal of both books will show that this charge is unfounded. Both writers drew their inspiration from the same source."[8]

As a matter of fact, la Avellaneda drew her information from several sources, including Bernal Díaz del Castillo, Solís, the letters of Cortez himself, Dr. Robertson, whom she highly praised, and Clavijero, whom she consulted on Aztec language and customs. She was quite proud of her scholarly diligence and wrote to Tassara in mid-April 1844 about the novel then being completed. She judges it to be good, and notes it has been admired by Martínez de la Rosa, Juan Nicasio Gallego, and Tassara's friend, Cárdenas. She expresses hope it will be published in a deluxe edition as well as in serial form in a newspaper, going on to talk about the care and effort which she has put into the preparation of the work: "que la autora ha hecho un estudio profundo de la conquista, del estado de la civilización azteca, del carácter de Cortés y compañía, apreciando con imparcialidad y exactitud los hechos y las circunstancias . . ." ("that the author has made a profound study of the history of the conquest, of the state of Aztec civilization, of the character of Cortez and his men, considering the facts and the circumstances with impartiality and exactitude . . .").[9] She adds that she polished and repolished her style so that the work would stand with the best historical novels.

At the same time that she proudly proclaims her careful research and authenticity, she speaks of the work as a "una novela semipoema" ("semipoetic novel"), and thus in a sense belies her own assertions. While there is much that is undoubtedly accurate in both events and descriptions, a large portion of the work is fiction invented by la Avellaneda to give the book a narration beyond the facts of history. As in *Espatolino*, Gertrudis utilizes history to convey her own message and views on life. There is also the tender love affair of the young Spaniard, Velázquez de León, with Tecuixpa, daughter of Montezuma, and the domestic love of the Princess Gualcazinla for her husband Cuauhtemoc.

La Avellaneda's sympathies clearly lie with the doomed but noble Aztecs rather than with the Spanish conquerors. The author glosses over the early life of Cortez and rapidly moves the action to the encounter with Montezuma. She portrays Cortez in a reasonably favorable light, but shows him as a cold, calculating, and pragmatic figure, hardly attractive as a human being. She says of him that "Los medios siempre eran para él cosas accesorias, y persuadíase con facilidad de su justicia siempre que tocase su utilidad. . . . Aconsejábale su política respetar la vida de Moctezuma; pero dictábale igualmente mantener y aumentar el terror, que podía únicamente allanarle el camino de la conquista" ("The means were always accessory things for him, and he persuaded himself easily of their justification as long as they were of utility. ... His political sense counseled him to respect Montezuma's life; but it also dictated to him to maintain and increase the terror as well, which was the only thing that could smooth the road to conquest"), (*OB* V, 238).

As was the case with Prescott, whose *History of the Conquest of Mexico* was published in the United States in 1843, la Avellaneda presents Montezuma in a sympathetic and appealing light. More than half of her story is concerned with him. He is portrayed as a man who inspired both respect and fear, who had given proof of his capacities as a ruler and of his bravery as a warrior. Tula writes of him: "Era liberal, magnífico, justiciero: sus parciales le atribuían una sabiduría sobrehumana y virtudes sublimes: sus enemigos le temían porque conocían su rigor y la violencia de sus resentimientos" ("He was liberal, magnificent, righteous; his partisans attributed superhuman wisdom and sublime virtues to him; his enemies feared him because they recognized his rigor and the violence of his resentments"), (*OB* V, 217). For all his strength, however, Montezuma is predestined for death and destruction. The gods have foreordained the end of the Aztec Empire, and it is the acceptance of this that deeply affects the actions of the emperor in his relations with Cortez and the Spanish invaders. Were these white men the descendants of the god Quetzalcoatl who have returned to claim their heritage? This is the dilemma, and faced by the strangers, the leaders vacillate, are divided, and finally conquered.

Tula's partiality is apparent throughout the novel, but is perhaps best exemplified in the conversations which Cortez has with Guacolando, the oldest and wisest of Montezuma's counselors. Cortez questions the old man about the laws and customs of the Aztecs. Guacolando replies that there are no written laws, as they believe that there should be no absolute laws; a certain flexibility is necessary, as one does not always know all possible cases that may occur. Consequently, the monarch is given the right to alter custom when justice requires it, and he must share this responsibility with his ministers and the nobles, and with tribunals in the capital cities of the provinces. Capital punishment does exist for several crimes: robbery without proven need, rebellion or disrespect toward the emperor, heresy, corruption in ministers or public servants, adultery, murder, and continuous drunkenness. There were also serious penalties for incest, crimes against chastity, and cowardice on the field of battle. Slavery was not hereditary, and all Mexicans were born free. For slaves, there was adequate justice and protection from excesses and mistreatment. Even Montezuma shows consideration for a subject who asks to see him alone to avoid individual embarrassment.

The negative side of the picture is omitted. Tula could not have carefully read her sources without full knowledge of the repression that the Aztecs had carried everywhere that their armies went, or the horribly cruel religious practices that required the constant "feeding" of the gods with the still-beating hearts of their victims. Gertrudis does mention the temple of the war god Huitzilipochtli, but there is no reference to the rites of cutting out the hearts of hundreds and even thousands of prisoners, of the stench of blood or the matted hair and the bloody uniforms of the priests that so repulsed and shocked the Spaniards, and which Bernal Díaz forcefully describes.

The novel ends on a note of madness, death, and of love. Gualcazinla, widow of the murdered Cuauhtemoc, in the madness of her grief, tries to kill Cortez, but doña Marina, the Indian princess who was his interpreter and mistress, historically, saves him. By this time, Cortez has given Marina a Spanish husband, but her love for Cortez transcends the marriage vows of both. Her love is great enough to justify adultery or even the murder of Gualcazinla, and she will lie to hide their guilt. She tells Cortez that he is her god, the center of greatness, wisdom, and heroism. "Yo no soy más que eso: una mujer loca por ti" ("I am no more than this: a woman who is crazy from love for you"), (*OB* V, 566). Tula concludes the work with a brief quotation from the chronicler Bernal Díaz del Castillo—who was with Cortez during the conquest—on the basis of which she invented the final scene of the novel. Tula herself had been a woman in love at the time she was writing *Cuauhtemoc*. The affair with Tassara was a kind of madness, and she had defied convention with tragic results.

Was doña Marina's declaration meant for Tassara? Ironically, the affair was over by the time of the book's publication. Tula's gods of love all proved to have feet of clay.

VIII   Dolores, Páginas de una crónica de familia

La Avellaneda's next full-length novel was entitled *Dolores, Páginas de una crónica de familia* (*Dolores, Pages from a Family Chronicle*). First published in the *Semanario Pintoresco* of Madrid in 1851, it was reissued in Havana in the paper *Diario de la Marina* in 1860. It was also published in book form in Mexico in 1891. The story is purportedly based on historical facts, but an examination of Tula's supposed sources indicates that the tale is one that Gertrudis invented, utilizing some historical figures to give credence to her claims of authenticity.

As in the case of *Munio Alfonso*, Tula's choice of subject matter reflects her pride in her paternal ancestry. *Dolores* is supposedly the story of one of her ancestors in the Middle Ages. The novel opens on January 12, 1425, the day of the baptism of the first-born son of King Juan II of Castille and his wife doña María de Aragón. The use of specific names, including doña Beatriz de Avellaneda, of detailed descriptions, and of the date, give a strong feeling of reality, which was what Gertrudis wished. She succinctly declares that not only Dolores, but all of the characters in the work, are historically real and are taken from a chronicle of the period: "Dolores, mi estimado amigo, existió realmente, como todos los personajes de esta historia, que parece novela, y cuyos principales hechos hallará usted en las crónicas de aquel tiempo." ("Dolores, my dear friend, really existed, as did all of the characters of this story, which appears to be a novel, and whose principal events you can find in the chronicles of that time.")[10] She wrote to the director of the *Semanario Pintoresco* that she had invented nothing, and that there had been no need to force her imagination in telling of "la extraña y dolorosa historia de aquella pobre criatura que existió realmente, como todos los personajes que en torno de ella se agrupan en este breve cuadro..." ("the strange and painful story of that poor creature who really existed, as did all of the persons who gather around her in this brief sketch...").[11]

Why Gertrudis insisted on the veracity of her story to such an
extent is something about which we can only speculate. Cotoreli
y Mori states just as categorically that no such person as Dolores
exists in the chronicles of the fifteenth century: "En primer lugar
la tal Dolores no ha existido nunca, ni semejante nombre se halla
en familia alguna del siglo XV. Conócense perfectamente los de
todos los hijos e hijas del primer Conde de Castro, y no hay
ninguna llamada Dolores" ("In the first place, the supposed
Dolores never existed, nor is any such name to be found in any
family in the fifteenth century. All of the names of the sons and
daughters of the first count of Castro are perfectly well known,
and there is no one called Dolores").[12] He concludes that we
must consider the work as nothing more than a novel freely
invented by the author.

The work revolves around several of Tula's favorite themes:
love at first sight thwarted by parental interference, the cruelty of
social position and custom that destroys the natural instincts of
youth, and the dangers of exaggerated pride and snobbery. The
mother figure, doña Beatriz de Avellaneda, is a monstrous woman,
ready and willing to go to any lengths to maintain what she
considers the honor and position of her family and rank. Dolores,
her sixteen-year-old daughter, has fallen in love with don Rodrigo
de Luna, the nephew of King Juan II's controversial minister don
Alvaro de Luna. Knowing that this is a love match, and intending
to satisfy the desires of his favorite don Alvaro as well as the
young couple, the king tells Dolores's father, don Diego Gómez
de Sandoval, the count of Castro-Xériz, that he has chosen don
Rodrigo to take his daughter's hand in marriage. When doña
Beatriz learns of the proposed match, she declares that she would
rather see her daughter dead than married to a member of the
Luna family, whom she considers upstarts. The father, seeing
how deeply his child loves the man the king has chosen for her,
pleads in vain with his implacable wife.

As a result of the conflict between her parents, Dolores has
convulsions and is confined to bed. A Doctor Yáñez is brought in
to care for her, and doña Beatriz meets in secret to talk with him.
The doctor tells the worried father that there is no possibility of
Dolores getting married, as she is far too ill. Shortly thereafter,
Dolores worsens and dies; instead of a wedding, there is a burial.

Doña Beatriz betrays no sign of loss or grief, but quickly withdraws from society, isolating herself with the old nurse of Dolores and her personal servant in a remote castle in the north that belongs to her husband. Even her husband hears from her only very irregularly.

Finally, after six years, the count visits the castle and there learns from the old nurse, who lives in terror of doña Beatriz, that his daughter is still alive, that she, like Shakespeare's Juliet, had been given a potion that made her appear to be dead. In the interim years, the hateful mother had kept her locked away from the world. Don Rodrigo, her would-be husband, has become a priest, and so the hoped-for union can never be. Dolores asks her father to take her to a convent, where she becomes an exemplary nun. Before leaving the castle, however, she persuades her father to forgive her mother and the sinister Isabel Pérez, who had been the accomplice in carrying out doña Beatriz's inhuman scheme. Rodrigo, who has become the archbishop of Santiago, frequents Dolores's supposed grave and weeps for her.

Given Tula's insistence on the truth of the story, we can wonder to what extent it was a projection of her own rejection of suitors that her family had chosen for her, or of problems with her own mother over her love affairs with Cepeda and Tassara. The portrayal of the mother borders on the grotesque, and the author at several points tries to mitigate her monstrousness through the gentle and forgiving love of the daughter. There is sound reason to identify the Dolores of the novel with reality, though not with that of the fifteenth century. Dolores lived in the nineteenth century: Gertrudis' full baptismal name was María Gertrudis de los Dolores. The name chosen for the protagonist was the author's own.

IX El artista barquero o los cuatro cinco de junio

The last full-length novel that la Avellaneda wrote was *El artista barquero o los cuatro cinco de junio* (*The Artist Boatman or the Fourth Fifths of June*). It was written in Cuba and published there in 1861. The author added that the novel was founded on an "anecdote" in the life of a well-known man, thus establishing once more a sense of reality and verisimilitude.

Several characters are historical figures: Hubert Robert, the artist of the title who is the protagonist, Madame de Pompadour, and Louis XV. The well-known man of the "anecdote" was Robert de Montesquieu—whom we know la Avellaneda greatly admired —the secret protector of Hubert Robert in his youthful efforts to make his way as an artist. Cotoreli y Mori sees it as the best of Tula's novels, but criticizes it somewhat as being too similar to works by Dumas Père.[13]

The story takes place in France in 1752, and in three successive years, the young Hubert Robert has to work as a boatman in Marseille to help his destitute mother and sister in the absence of his father. A stranger gives him a purse of gold, which he thinks is a mistake, but is unable to find the owner. He meets and falls in love with a lovely Creole named Josefina, who is from Cuba and lives with her father and a Cuban servant, Niná. They meet on the fifth of June, and their story—or rather that of Hubert —continues for the next three years to give the "four fifths of June" of the title. Josefina and Niná's love of Cuba and their reminiscences of it suggest more than fiction. Josefina is another semiportrait of the author herself in her youth, while the story of Josefina's parents' deep love is a rare instance of marital love whose intensity rivals that of the frustrated figures who people the pages of Tula's other works, whether in novelistic or in play form. A little temple in the garden of the parents' home in Cuba was the symbol of their love and the happiness that was brought to a tragic end with the death of the wife in childbirth at the age of thirty. The father, a Frenchman named Caillard, who has become bitter and materialistic, forbids Josefina to see any more of the impecunious boatman, who he thinks has no future, no name, and no money.

Hubert's father does return, and Hubert goes off to Paris to study at the expense of an unknown benefactor. Tula uses the opportunity to describe the Paris which she herself knew and visited, the Paris of Louis Philippe, comparing it to the eighteenth-century Paris in which the story develops. A sketch of Hubert catches the eye of none other than King Louis XV's mistress, the famous Madame de Pompadour, historically one of the greatest patrons of the arts of all time. Through her, Hubert goes to the Elysée Palace—built as a residence for Madame de Pompa-

dour and now the official residence of the president of France—
and to the Chateau of Versailles. Louis XV is a refined and
polished version of the Baltasar of Tula's play: the elegant balls,
the hunting parties, and the great banquets do little to alleviate
his boredom and tedium. Madame de Pompadour also suffers
from the artificiality and emptiness of court life. She has, she confides to Hubert, never really loved. Like the Countess Catalina of
Two Women, she seems an assured and triumphant citizen of the
world, but in essence is a woman in search of love and meaning
for her life. She is a public figure who wants private happiness,
the cosmopolitan woman with every luxury and comfort, who
longs for the simple life with the man she loves! Tula tells us
that "En sus horas de felicidad, habría creído poder purificarse
por el amor verdadero" ("In her hours of happiness, she would
have thought it possible to purify herself by a true love") (*OB* IV,
150). When Hubert hears that Josefina is engaged to marry
someone else, he is ready to give himself to Madame de Pompadour, but his illness prevents their love from being any more
than the unattainable dream of the magnanimous marchioness.

Hubert does win Josefina's hand. He paints the ideal picture of
the temple of love that Monsieur Caillard has sought so long as
a remembrance of his marriage, the supposed fiancé breaks off
the engagement, and the wedding takes place in the presence of
the generous Pompadour at the Palace of Versailles on the fourth
fifth of June. During the banquet celebrating the wedding,
Hubert learns that his benefactor was Montesquieu. The novel
ends with the death of Pompadour. Only Hubert Robert truly
mourns his noble but unhappy friend as her body is secretly
taken away from Versailles on a dark rainy day. The pomp and
circumstances that had surrounded her in life meant less than the
moments of generosity and affection that her friendship for
Hubert had brought her.

Pompadour and Josefina are two sides of a single portrait, just
as Countess Catalina and Luisa constitute a fictional self-portrait
of the successful but basically unhappy and neurasthenic Tula,
in middle-age still nostalgic for the innocent happiness of the
past, but fully aware of the fugitive nature of honors and fame.
Both Catalina and Pompadour end their lives without real fulfillment, but they are far more interesting and believable than the

insipid ingenues who are their rivals and are little more than stereotypes of the romantic heroine that even in la Avellaneda's first novel, *Sab*, could not stand the test of time and real life.

CHAPTER 5

Shorter Prose Works

IN addition to the full-length novels, la Avellaneda also wrote shorter prose works, some of which she herself called legends (*leyendas*) and others which would be classified as either long short stories, or short novels. Although these are stories which the author tells us are not original with her, she manages in every case to give the narrative an orientation and thematic development of her own. There is also the lengthy article on women ("La mujer") which offers a cogent argument for the rights and dignity of women, travel articles describing a trip to northern Spain and southern France shortly after Colonel Verdugo's recovery from the stabbing incident, and the love letters (*cartas amorosas*) of Gertrudis to Cepeda which have been published separately from the fictional works and poetry.

I *The Letters to Cepeda*

The love letters which la Avellaneda wrote to don Ignacio de Cepeda over a period of fifteen years, from 1839 to 1854, are, as previously noted, a major source of autobiographical and psychological information. Without them, any study of the author's works would be considerably diminished. As they frequently parallel her fiction or are repeated almost word for word in the plays, novels, and poems, they provide us with a key to a deeper comprehension of certain passages and scenes that might otherwise provoke only speculation. They make the reasons for Tula's vain insistence that the opening of *Leoncia* be postponed so that Cepeda could be present, understandable and cogent. Leoncia's tortured love was the transformation to stage fiction of Gertrudis's and Cepeda's drama of love. The

157

verbal expressions of the countess's passion in *Two Women* can
also be considered an extension of the letters, a release of the
torrent of feeling that if personally expressed would have undoubtedly deepened the rift between Tula and her reticent and
provincially conservative lover.

The letters also provide a source of information about Tula's
life, doings, and interests. The autobiographical sketch in the
form of a letter which Gertrudis wrote on the night of July 29,
1839, is frequently drawn upon for information concerning the
author and her family's early life. In other letters she discusses
her readings and her writings and includes portions of poems,
but above all she tries to maintain—whether under the guise of
love or friendship—something of the precarious and fluctuating
relationship between herself and Cepeda. We know from the
ruptures that she did not always succeed. Some of the breaks
were lengthy, but the correspondence begins once more, even
on days when the two had seen each other during Cepeda's stay
in Madrid, until Cepeda's marriage.

The story of the survival and publication of the letters is a
curious one. Tula's last letter to Cepeda, dated March 26, 1854,
gives a clue to what happened. Although Cepeda repeatedly
withdrew from the relationship with Tula, only to return again
and to tantalize her over the years, he was clearly aware of what
a famous and extraordinary woman Gertrudis was. The final lines
of Tula's last letter to him address themselves to the body of
letters that she had sent him. She states that she does not remember whether there are things of a confidential nature in
them or not that might be of interest to the public, or whether
they should be kept private: ("Ignoro si hay en esas cartas
confidenciales cosas que puedan interesar al público, o si las
hay de tal naturaleza que deban ser reservadas").[1] Nevertheless,
Cepeda kept fifty-three letters, and in his will, requested that
his widow have them printed at his expense. They were published in 1907, a year after his death.[2] Ironically, the name of
Cepeda, which was never to be Tula's through marriage, has
attained a fame and immortality through her that it never would
have had otherwise.

Not every line of the letters is lyrical, but there are passages
of great poetic beauty, deeply felt and deeply moving. We can

only speculate on the attraction of this man who inspired them and who was to hold emotional sway over Tula for so many years. Tula herself asks the question: "¿Quién eres? ¿Qué poder es ése? ¿Quién te lo ha dado? Tú no eres un hombre, no, a mis ojos. Eres el Angel de mi destino, y pienso muchas veces al verte que te ha dado el mismo Dios el poder supremo de dispensarme los bienes y males que debo gozar y sufrir en este suelo" ("Who are you? What power is this? Who gave it to you? You are not a man, no, not in my eyes. You are the angel of my destiny, and I often think when I see you that God Himself has given you the supreme power to allot me the pleasures and pains that I must enjoy and suffer on this earth"), (*AN*, 104). So much of la Avellaneda's life and career is tied to the pain and frustration that came of her love that we wonder what would have happened if she had become Cepeda's wife; would she have had a literary career beyond perhaps the writing of a few poems?

II *Articles on Women*

La Avellaneda's interest in the position of women in society, in the literary world, and in private life, was a major and enduring concern, appearing again and again as a central theme of her plays, prose works, and even certain poems. Her pioneering spirit in this sensitive area and her daring outspokenness undoubtedly had much to do with the criticisms, faultfinding, and slanderous gossip of which she was a constant object. Compared with the statements and situations in the fictional works, the article which she wrote and published in Cuba "La mujer" ("Woman"), in 1860, is a relatively muted and innocuous document. It nevertheless attempts to question women's status before a Hispanic public, and as such is of interest in the light of stronger women's movements of today.

In la Avellaneda's plays and novels, woman is the victim of inflexible social codes that define her role without regard for her feelings or abilities. One heroine after another ends in suicide or madness, the only recourses open to them in a society which affords women no freedom of action. The article on women, surprisingly enough, makes aggressive mention only of the exclusivity of the Royal Spanish Academy, for which Tula still felt rancor. Her exclusion from that prestigious group of men was obviously something that she could neither forget nor forgive. She particularly mentions the patriotism of women, some of whom have made notable sacrifices for their countries. Despite this, she says, women are not permitted to take part in public affairs. The rest of the article, a fairly long one, is devoted to a discussion of women and religion, the strength and importance of love and feeling—in which women are superior to men—and a listing and presentation of the accomplishments of a series of well-known women, dating from those of pagan antiquity, through the Virgin Mary, Joan of Arc, Isabella the Catholic, and including a brief but laudatory mention of her contemporary, George Sand. The power of the heart and of sentiments more than balances the physical strength and intellectual potential of men.

"La mujer," in the final analysis, cannot be considered as much more than a rather tepid reflection of the passionate case for women's dignity and freedom that her earlier works contain, but by 1860 la Avellaneda was ill, disillusioned, and desirious of avoiding controversy. The major periods of her creativity were over. The extraordinary vitality of the previous two decades was coming to an end.

III   *Short Prose Fiction*

All of the shorter fictional pieces that la Avellaneda wrote may be classified as legends (*leyendas*) inasmuch as they are based on folk traditions that had survived down to the nineteenth century in local oral form. Tula supposedly heard them from guides or from an old man of an area she was visiting—a common literary device of the period for the remaking of these folk tales in written form. With the exception of her last two legends, the others (seven) included in her complete works are set in the Jura Mountains of France—"La Baronesa de Joux" ("The Baroness of Joux"), 1844—and in Switzerland—"La velada del helecho o El donativo del diablo" ("The Vigil of the Fern Plant or the Gift of the Devil"), 1849; "La montaña maldita" ("The Mountain of the Mother's Curse"), 1850; "La dama de Amboto" ("The Lady of Amboto"), written in 1858; "La bella Toda y los doce jabalíes" ("The Beautiful Toda and the Twelve Wild Boars"), 1858; "La flor del ángel" ("The Angel's Flower"), 1859; and "La ondina del lago azul" ("The Water Nymph of the Blue Lake"), 1859. Several of these were reprinted in the *Album cubano* that Tula founded and directed in Cuba in 1860.

All belong to the tradition of medieval folk tales and center either on a ruined castle or on a place that la Avellaneda has visited, or that she has been told about. Her brother Manuel, for example, recounted the Swiss legends to her, but she herself heard the stories of the Basque regions and the Pyrenees while traveling in the north of Spain and south of France with her second husband, Verdugo. The tales are peopled with satanic figures and their victims for the most part, and might well be categorized as tales of terror and the supernatural, being clearly within the traditions of romantic medievalism and the gothic novel which gave us such figures as Dracula. The people or guides who relate these stories to la Avellaneda are as superstitious as the characters in the tales themselves. One of the legends, with the title *The Gift of the Devil*, was transformed, as seen in the chapter on drama, into a full-length play that opened in 1852.

The legend of "The Baroness de Joux" is based on a short poem by a French poet named Demesnay. The son of a tyrannical father, Baron Amauri inherits great wealth. He is determined to have the hand of Berta of Luneville, although she has been betrothed to the heir of the Montfaucon family as a means of ending a feud between the two families. Amauri rekindles the animosity between the two families, and obtains Berta in marriage. She still loves Montfaucon, however, and while her husband is away on the Second Crusade, she falls seriously ill until a wondering troubadour—Aimer de Montfaucon in disguise—comes to her and cares for her. When Amauri returns, Lothario, an old servant, tells his master that his honor has been besmirched. Amauri, in revenge, murders Montfaucon and presents his severed head to his horrified wife in a mosaic coffer he has brought her as a gift from the Holy Land. No one knows of the murder, only that Aimer has disappeared. Berta sickens, supposedly dies, and is buried before anyone can even see the corpse. Not long after, sounds of lamentation fill the castle.

When servants finally go to the depths of the dungeons beneath the castle, they see a headless ghost. Berta's old nurse Alicia speculates that her mistress did not die, but was imprisoned in a dungeon until she did die.

"The Mountain of the Mother's Curse," like the other Swiss legend, was one that Manuel de Avellaneda told his sister. It is a story that contains little that we associate with Tula's interests, except that she makes the mother a woman who has sinned and been abandoned by her seducer. Her illegitimate son, Walter Muller, is an only child on whom the mother has lavished every care and tenderness. The story takes place after the son is full grown, and has become a rich farmer. His mother has lived apart from him in humble lodgings, while he, in his opulence, has built a fine house for himself and a special barn—called a palace by the local farmers—for his favorite animal, a white calf. Whatever symbolic value or psychological implications all of this may have had, la Avellaneda does nothing to exploit them, merely stating the above in a fairly brief outline, before proceeding to the climax of her tale. The mother has lost all she had and comes to the son to beg him to take her in, but Muller will have nothing to do with her. After a violent quarrel in which the son orders the mother to leave his house, despite a gathering night's snowstorm, the mother places a curse on Walter Muller and all of his belongings. She goes out into the night and begins to descend the mountain toward the valley. There is a horrendous roar, and the mountain collapses, completely engulfing Muller and all of his farm. The next morning, the mother's body is found and given burial, but the earth of Muller's lost estates remains forever sterile.

"The Lady of Amboto" also a medieval legend, set in the Basque country through which Tula was traveling, is the story of a fratricide. A beautiful daughter born to the family of the Urraca's grows up an only child and the sole heir to vast estates, but her widowed father marries a second time. A son is born, and since the line of succession can only be to a female if there is no male heir, the unhappy María becomes dependent on her brother.

During a hunting party, María rides off alone in pursuit of a wounded boar. Her white horse disappears, and don Pedro, the brother, follows her to protect her. Meanwhile, a terrible storm begins. Everyone goes back to the castle to await the return of brother and sister, but only María reappears. The following day, the bloody body of don Pedro is found at the bottom of a precipice. His horse's neck had been pierced through by a javelin. With his death María inherits all of the estates, but she is not happy, and becomes more and more ill. On the anniversary of the death of don Pedro, while all of the servants are at prayer for the dead man's soul, María seems more ill than ever, and Tula describes the tainted beauty of the ailing noblewoman. As a storm breaks, María has a ghostly hallucination, rushes out into the night, and is not seen again until her body is discovered in the same chasm where her brother's had been found. She has committed suicide, but her ghost is condemned to walk the earth as atonement for her fratricide.

The two legends which Tula published together, "The Beautiful Toda" and "The Twelve Wild Boars," are also from the Basque region of northern Spain. The first story is based on a little-known anecdote involving an adulterous love affair of King Ferdinand of Aragón with the young and beautiful Toda de Larrea. On the orders of Queen Isabella, the errant Toda and the lovely daughter born of her love affair, are sent to a convent. There, several years later, after the mother's death, the angelic and unfortunate daughter is to be made abbess. King Ferdinand comes for the ceremony, but his daughter, a loyal subject, can only kiss her father's hand. The second legend of Vizcaya recounts the love of don Juan de Avedaño and his wife Elvira. The husband has awakened the jealousy of the prince by his prowess as a horseman, and Elvira has made an enemy of the prince's favorite, Lazama, whose hand she rejected. Both prince and rejected suitor plan revenge. A public fight against five wild boars is staged in the public plaza. The prince is thrown from his horse but Avedaño goes into the ring and kills one of the boars. His triumph is short-lived. That very night, Lazama's henchmen come to the castle, and despite Elvira's entreaties, Avedaño admits them to his rooms. They murder him and throw his corpse over a balcony to the ravenous boars who wait below to devour his body. Elvira flees to a convent with Avedaño's infant son, and refuses Lazama's offers of marriage. The son, with cruel irony, is conceded the use of twelve golden wild boars in his coat of arms.

"The Angel's Flower" is a love story which Tula herself compares to the famed tale of the lovers of Teruel. Rosa, who is fifteen, wants to marry Félix Erliá, who is eighteen. The father opposes the match because Félix is too poor, but agrees finally to give him three years in which to make his fortune. The two lovers part when Félix sets out for the New World. They look at the angel flower and the bee, and vow to be as deeply united. Rosa, however, is told by a sea captain that Félix has married someone else, and, in her disappointment, she accepts the hand of an older man. Shortly thereafter, Félix returns, too late. Félix falls ill and dies of consumption and, soon after, Rosa also dies. The kind husband has the two lovers buried side by side so that they may be united in death as they could not be in this life.

"The Water Nymph of the Blue Lake" is, as already mentioned, a variation of the well-known legend on which Gustavo Adolfo Bécquer based his more famous version entitled "Los ojos verdes" ("The Green Eyes"). Up to a certain point, both authors' versions are quite close. Tula meets a "tió Santiago" through her guide, and hears the story of Gabriel, the last surviving son of the old man, and of the blue lake that they are visiting. "Uncle Santiago" had lost three sons when Gabriel was born. He took good care of him and gave him an excellent education. The youth was angelically handsome and by the age of eighteen was a musician who could play the flute, write both music and poetry, sing, and speak several languages. An avid reader of works from France and Germany, as well as Spain, he sought poetry in the beauty of nature, drawing sustenance from it. It was this youth who became enthralled with the nymph of the blue eyes that inhabited the depths of the blue lake. Fascinated by the soft murmur of her voice and by the hypnotic spell of her blue eyes, he finally joined her in the dark blue waters. Only his flute is found beside the lake.

Lorenzo the guide tells the story as a folk tale, and questions the superstition of the people who believe the legend. He goes to Paris, however, and through a friend sees a very beautiful woman with blue eyes in the Bois de Boulogne. He asks who the woman is and is told that she is a widowed countess, one of the most attractive and sought-after women in Paris, and the most flirtatious and capricious. For the past three years she has gone to the valley by the blue lake in the Pyrenees where "convirtió aquellos lugares agrestes en brillante teatro de aventuras maravillosas, dignas de figurar en las mil y una noches" ("she converted those rustic places into the brilliant theater of marvellous adventures, worthy of being included in the thousand and one nights"), (*OB* V, 690). Lorenzo asks la Avellaneda later on if she does not agree with him that it is preferable to retain the belief in the story of the water nymph of the blue lake rather than to suspect of the countess a heartless disdain that would have brought Gabriel to suicide. Tula strongly agrees, affirming that this is a far better explanation than to suppose that the countess has been cruelly incapable of responding to the artistic sensitivities of the young man who threw himself into the lake.

IV *Two American Legends*

The two legends based on material drawn from American history were written in Cuba in 1860 or 1861, and not published until several years later. The first one, "El aura blanca" ("The White Vulture"), is quite short and is based on a story of Gertrudis's own home city of Puerto Príncipe in Cuba. The action recounted took place in Tula's youth.

A monk of the Franciscan order, called Father Valencia by the townspeople, was beloved for his charity and good works. Whenever there were problems, whether domestic, business, or of other kinds, Father Valencia was always helpful. He exemplified the best of Christian kindness. There was only one problem about which he could do nothing: the lepers who roamed the streets begging, whose number grew almost daily. Father Valencia comforted them as best he could, but finally took a beggar's basket and went through the town from door to door asking for alms to build a leper's hospital. Despite what seemed like an impossibility, the good monk realized his dream. A hospital was built, and Father Valencia was the director of it.

Several years of very bad times came, however. The number of beggars increased, and even those townspeople comfortably well off could not give to the support of the hospital as they had before. Many lepers had to leave, passing by the tomb of their now-dead benefactor to shed their tears and to pray over his ashes. They lived in the gardens of the hospital that had previously sheltered them and lamented the fact that the tropical birds that had once come to eat bread at their feet came no more. Only the vultures lurked nearby awaiting their deaths.

At this point, Tula interrupts her story to give a description of the typical Cuban vulture or *aura* in all of its repugnance. The day of the event, however, a white vulture appeared, alike in form to the others, but pure white like a swan and with rose-colored beak and claws. Its eyes were as soft as a dove's. When it came to earth the other vultures flew away in fright, but it was tame and let itself be held by the lepers who said that it was the soul of their beloved Father Valencia come to comfort them. When the townspeople heard the story, they began to contribute to the hospital again. The white vulture in a golden cage was shown throughout the island, and people contributed to a new period of prosperity and confidence in the Hospital of Saint Lazarus.

The other story, long enough to be classified as a short novel, is set in New Granada—now Colombia in South America—in the second half of the sixteenth century. Its protagonist, the chieftain or *cacique* of the title "El Cacique de Tumerqué," is the son of one of the original conquistadors and an Indian princess. At the time the story begins, King Philip II has sent an official to Bogotá to investigate abuses and corruption among persons in authority. The official is don Juan Bautista Monzón, and he arrives in Santa Fe de Bogotá in the year 1579. After investigations, he dismisses several corrupt officials and thereby earns their enmity. The treasurer, don Alonso de Orozco, remains more or less neutral in the struggle that develops until Monzón interfers in his personal life. Orozco had been having an adulterous affair with the beautiful wife of an army captain, one of the most attractive women of the land, named Estrella. As la Avellaneda describes her, Estrella is not an evil or a callous woman, but one who, lacking a proper education and being addicted to the highly romanticized novels of chivalry, idealized first her prosaic husband, and then the equally uninteresting Orozco.

The latter proves to be dangerously vengeful. She is incapable of separating dream from reality, and consequently entered into the adulterous affair.

It is Orozco's wife who precipitates a crisis, going to Monzón to demand that something be done to protect her and her reputation. Monzón visits Estrella's house and there orders her to leave with her husband who is being sent on duty to Turmerqué. There Estrella meets and falls in love with the handsome chieftain, the cacique of Tumerqué, whose Spanish name is don Diego de Torres. He returns her love, but on the night of their first tryst in the garden of Estrella's home, Orozco, who has come to Tumerqué in disguise and has seen the cacique and Estrella talking together at a hunting party, surprises the two. He and don Diego fight a duel. The black slave who is Estrella's *confidante* finds blood on the garden walk and so knows that one of the two men has been wounded. Finally, Estrella learns that it was Orozco who had almost died from his wounds, but who was nursed back to health thanks to don Diego's good offices.

In the meantime, Monzón, noting Orozco's strange absence from Bogotá, sends a trusted servant, Juan Roldán, to find Orozco. Roldán learns the truth of the dueling incident and, shortly thereafter, Orozco returns to the capital. Soon rumors circulate throughout the city that an uprising is being planned by the Indians against the Spaniards, with the cacique supposedly the leader. Monzón, realizing what Orozco is trying to do to his rival by starting such rumors, sends Roldán to warn don Diego to leave at once for Spain, but the latter is overly confident. He writes a letter to Monzón telling him that there is nothing to fear, as he can easily gather together a large force of men loyal to him. When Roldán is waylaid by henchmen of Orozco on his return to Bogotá, the letter is taken and proves sufficiently ambiguous to bring about the cacique's arrest, imprisonment, and sentence of death. Only through Roldán's cleverness is don Diego able to escape from his prison cell. He flees to his countrymen who hide him among the peasant workers. There, by accident, he and Estrella are together again. Their love grows, but when the time is ripe, don Diego leaves for the coast and boards a ship for Spain to plead his innocence before the king.

Roldán, meanwhile, is arrested and put to torture. Despite

the horrors of pain that he is subjected to, he does not confess the part that Monzón had played in the escape of the cacique. Estrella, however, is betrayed by her Negro slave. Her husband, saying nothing, takes her back to Tumerqué from the country house where she had been staying. She falls ill when her husband, in a test of her feelings, tells her falsely that don Diego has been lost at sea. A physician is called in to bleed her, supposedly to death to satisfy her husband's honor, but the latter relents when he sees her blood, and he touches the wound. Shortly thereafter, the beautiful Estrella dies, possibly poisoned when her husband touched her open wound.

The story ends when the captain, who has gone to Spain to avenge his honor against the two men who were his wife's lovers, learns that revenge is best left to heaven. He finds that Orozco has gone mad and that the cacique has put his knowledge of horses and horsemanship to work in the service of King Philip, from whom he receives only a very small wage. Both men have atoned for their sins by the force of circumstance. The moral of the story is that it is best to forgive, to forget, and to leave vengeance to Heaven's dictates.

"The Cacique of Tumerqué" is one of those shorter writings of la Avellaneda regarded in later years as a minor masterwork. It embodies much of what is important and typical throughout her works. As we can see from the plot outline, la Avellaneda includes many of her favorite themes: the idealistic and beautiful young woman who lives for love and who is brought to her death because of it; adultery and its social consequences and implications; social and legal justice; the horrors of physical torture as a means of forcing confession; the perfidy and fickleness of human beings; the dangers of jealousy and the importance of forgiveness of human foibles.

It is a fitting work to end our discussion of la Avellaneda's writings. Two more plays did come from her pen after she returned to Spain, and she accomplished the major undertaking of revising and editing her works for the collected edition of 1869–1872. However, neither of the plays are typical of her style, and neither of them, as mentioned earlier, were produced. Consequently, we can consider "The Cacique de Tumerqué" as her last original work of note, and it is a fitting ending to so extraordinary a career.

Notes and References

Chapter One

1. Various publications appeared at the time of the centennial celebrations in Havana in 1914. Some are reproduced in the reissue, in augmented form, of la Avellaneda's works. There are also lengthy quotations from the lavishly laudatory statements of Tula's contemporaries in the literary world of Spain. She is consistently hailed as one of the greatest women writers in the history of Spanish literature.

2. In the so-called autobiography which she wrote for Ignacio de Cepeda on July 29, 1839.

3. In Emilio Cotareli y Mori, *La Avellaneda y sus obras* (Madrid: Tipografía de Archivos, 1930), p. 15; taken from the autobiography of 1850. Cotareli's lengthy quotations from now inaccessible material and his careful documentation make his book very valuable. His opinions, however, are another matter.

4. Ibid., p. 15. Cotareli sees George Sand's influence as an early and decisive one, but does not give his source for this conclusion. Alberto J. Carlos, in his article "La Avellanedo y la mujer" in the *Actas del Tercer Congreso Internacional de Hispanistas* (México, D.F.: Colegio de México, 1970), pp. 187–193, makes a strong point for the influence of Madame de Staël rather than Sand in the writing of Tula's second novel, *Dos mujeres*. He affirms, however, la Avellaneda's reading of Sand, but sees her concepts concerning woman in society as coming from her own experience rather than her reading of her famous French contemporary.

5. These and other quotations and references are from the memoires (*memorias*) which la Avellaneda wrote to a cousin, Eloisa de Arteaga y Loinaz, in the form of notebooks (*cuadernillos*). They are based on diary notes as well as memory and are four in number. Three are dated November, 1838, and one December, 1838. Written in Seville, they constitute a kind of travel diary beginning with the crossing of the Atlantic in 1836, and including sections on the cities which la Avellaneda visited in her first two years in Europe: Bordeaux in France, La Coruña, Santiago de Compostela, Pontevedra and Vigo

169

in Galicia, Lisbon in Portugal, Cadiz and Seville in Andalusia. They are reproduced in their entirety in Domingo Figarola-Caneda, *Gertrudis Gómez de Avellaneda, Biografía, bibliografía e iconografía, incluyendo muchas cartas, inéditas o publicadas, escritas por la gran poetisa o dirigidas a ella, y sus memorias.* (Madrid: Sociedad General Española de Librería, 1929).

6. The details of this "affair" came to light in 1907 when the letters of la Avellaneda to Cepeda were published.

7. Cotareli y Mori, p. 37.

8. See Alberto López Arguëllo, *La Avellaneda y sus versos* (Santander, 1898), p. 12.

9. In Lorenzo Cruz de Fuentes, *La Avellaneda. Autobiografía y cartas* (Huelva: Miguel Mora, 1907), pp. 89–90.

10. Ibid.

11. Letter 11, written in October, 1839.

12. Letter 12.

13. Letter 16.

14. All of the poems cited are to be found in the 1869, 1914, and now, the 1974, editions of the *Obras,* in all of which the *Poesías* comprise the first volume. Page references are to the *Obras* from volume CCLXXII of the edition of the Biblioteca de Autores Españoles (Madrid: Ediciones Atlas, 1974). Volumes CCLXXVIII and CCLXXIX comprise tomes II and III of the Obras, and include the drama. They were published in 1978 and 1979, respectively. Presumably there will be either two or three more volumes comprising the novels and shorter prose works in the same series, all following the 1914 edition. "Amor y orgullo": *OB* I, pp. 267–269.

15. Cotareli y Mori, p. 62.

16. Prologue to the first edition of la Avellaneda's *Poesías,* 1841.

17. In the *Biografía,* edition of *Poesías,* 1850, xvi–xvii.

18. Cotareli y Mori, p. 89.

19. Ibid., p. 134 (letter 31).

20. Ibid., p. 141 (letter 32).

21. *Poesías,* 1850, pp. 227–235.

22. Entitled "A él," it appeared in the edition of 1850, and with slight changes in the *Poesías* of 1869.

23. These works were mentioned by Nicomedes Pastor Díaz, but must have been lost, as no such works by la Avellaneda have survived.

24. Cotareli y Mori, p. 197.

25. Ibid., pp. 231–240, includes long quotations from newspaper reviews of *La hija de las flores.*

26. Ibid., see pp. 241–254.

27. Letter 53.
28. The portrait is reproduced in Cotareli y Mori, facing p. 285.
29. Ibid., pp. 318–337 are devoted to the incident, a highly melo-dramatic affair that reads like a "dime novel."
30. Ibid., pp. 347–349. The list of dignitaries is of interest.
31. *Album Cubano de lo Bueno y lo Bello. Revista Quincenal. De Moral, Literatura, Bellas Artes y Modas. Dedicada al Bello Sexo y Dirigida por Doña Gertrudis G. de Avellaneda* (Havana: Estableci-miento Tipográfico La Antilla, 1860). Several months after finishing the writing of the present manuscript on la Avellaneda, I saw a copy of this very rare publication at the Librería Mirto in Madrid. A few days later, I received the *Album* as a gift from my dear friends Ramón Revuelta Benito and his wife María del Carmen Izuzquiza de Revuelta. It is an interesting publication, but shows a much more conventional Tula than the romantic figure of the early writings.
32. She describes this in a letter to don Luciano Pérez Acevedo, of August 18, 1863, reproduced in Figarola-Caneda, pp. 228–229.

Chapter Two

1. First published in Cruz de la Fuente.
2. Quoted in Raimundo Lazo, *Gertrudis Gómez de Avellaneda. La mujer y la poetisa lírica* (México, D.F.: Editorial Porrúa, 1972), p. 48: "yo tenía en mi cabeza un mundo que no era el mundo real. La vida y los hombres no se me daban a conocer tales cuales yo los imaginaba. Empezaba ya a padecer...." ("I had in my head a world that was not the real one. Life and men did not present them-selves to me as I imagined them. I began to suffer....")
3. Ibid., pp. 37–39.
4. Ibid., pp. 76–85.

Chapter Three

1. The histories of Spanish literature do not mention the play-writing of these two authors, but Melveena McKendrick, in her *Woman and Society in the Spanish Drama of the Golden Age, A Study of the Mujer Varonil* (London, 1974), states, p. 22, that "the two other women [doña María Carvajal y Saavedra and doña María de Zayas] were first and foremost story-writers, although both wrote plays which have not survived, and one was in addition 'the most famous poetess of her time'". According to another source, María de Sayas, *Novelas: La burlada Aminta y venganza del honor y El pre-venido engañado* (Madrid: Taurus, 1966), one of the plays of Zayas

has been identified among the many anonymous Golden Age works. Its title is *La traición de la amistad*. The introduction to that volume states, however,: "Dentro del panorama general del teatro español del siglo XVII no creemos ... que pueda asignarse a doña María un puesto eminente ..." ("Within the general panorama of Spanish theater of the seventeenth century we do not believe ... that an eminent place can be ceded to doña María ..."), p. 22. George Sand wrote some twenty-five plays, some for reading only, and others for performance at Nohant. She was far less successful as a playwright than as a novelist. Only a few of her plays had long runs. In addition to Sand, there is the curious case of a mother and daughter in nineteenth-century French literature who also wrote plays. The mother, Sophie (Michaud de la Lavalette) Gay (1776–1852), created light operas, comedies, and straight dramas. Her daughter, Delphine Gay Girardin (1804–1855), was the wife of the writer Emile de Girardin. She, like la Avellaneda, was a poet, novelist, and short-story writer, and does deserve the title of successful playwright. Between 1839 and the year of her death, she saw two tragedies and several comedies successfully produced on the Paris stage.

2. Professor Libuse Reed of Ohio Wesleyan University found information on both of the women playwrights, and two others while doing research in London. There is information about them. I give the following brief mention: Susanne Courtlivre (1670?–1723), and the titles of two plays: *The Busy Body* and *The Wonder: A Woman Who Keeps a Secret*; Aphra Behn (1640–1689) and the titles of four plays: *The Dutch Lover, The Debauchee, The Feign'd Curtizan,* and *The Rover*; Hannah Cowley (1743–1809) and the titles of three plays: *The Belle's Stratagem, A Bold Stroke for a Husband,* and *The Runaway*. A lesser English writer, Mary Pix (1666–1720?) also wrote plays.

3. *La verdad vence apariencias* opened in February, *Errores del corazón* in May, *El donativo del diablo,* which was not successful, in October, *La hija de las flores* also in October, and the short *loa* entitled *El héroe de Bailén* on which Tula collaborated.

4. In the centennial *Obras* (Havana: Imprenta de A. Miranda, 1914), III, p. 622. Further references will be to this edition of the *Obras*.

5. Ibid., p. 607.

6. Tula herself says this in the dedication to the tragedy *Munio Alfonso* in her *Obras*.

7. Several reviews of the play are reproduced in Cotareli y Mori, pp. 59–66.

8. In Cruz de Fuentes, p. 116.

9. In Edwin Bucher Williams, *The Life and Dramatic Works of Gertrudis Gómez de Avellaneda* (Philadelphia: The University of Pennsylvania, 1924), p. 24, quotes P. Francisco Blanco, and defends la Avellaneda's use of a fourth act. Williams discusses at length the changes that Tula made in the play before including it in the edition of the *Obras* of 1869–1871 which she prepared herself.

10. Ibid.

11. Discussed by Williams, pp. 37–39.

12. *Obras* II, p. 495: "por la enojosa y tenaz enfermedad que hace algún tiempo ataca mis nervios y mi cerebro."

13. Williams devotes pp. 59–60 to a discussion of the versions of Alfieri and Soumet.

14. Cotareli y Mori gives a detailed description of the events, pp. 347–49.

Chapter Four

1. The edition by Carmen Bravo Villasante (Salamanca: Biblioteca Anaya, 1970), contains an introduction and a brief bibliography as well as the text of the novel.

2. *Obras*, V, 7.

3. José Fernández Montesinos in his *Introducción a una historia de la novela en España en el siglo XIX* (Valencia: Editorial Castalia, 1955), devotes over a hundred pages, pp. 154–257, to a bibliography of translations of novels in Spain between 1800 and 1850.

4. All quotations from *Sab* refer to the edition of Bravo Villasante as it is relatively easy to obtain.

5. Cotareli y Mori, p. 75.

6. From: Fernando Portuondo del Prado, *Historia de Cuba* (Havana: Juan Fernández Burgos, 1957).

7. Cotareli y Mori gives this information on p. 109, but says almost nothing about the novel itself.

8. From the preface to *Cuauhtemoc, The Last Aztec Emperor, an Historical Novel by Gertrudis Gómez de Avellaneda,* trans. Mrs. Wilson W. Blake (Mexico City: F. P. Hoeck, 1898). Apparently the novel was a success in Mexico; Cotareli y Mori, p. 128, cites two editions in Spanish published there, one in 1853 and another in 1887.

9. Quoted in Mario Méndez Bejarano, *Tassara: Nueva biografía crítica* (Madrid: 1928), p. 42.

10. Prologue to the novel in the edition of *Obras* of 1869, reprinted in the centennial edition of 1914.

11. Reproduced in Cotareli y Mori, p. 201.
12. Ibid., p. 203.
13. Ibid., p. 353.

Chapter Five

1. Gertrudis Gómez de Avellaneda, *Antología, poesías y cartas amorosas. Prólogo y edición de Ramón Gómez de la Serna* (Buenos Aires: Espasa Calpe, 1945), p. 149.

2. In the original edition that Cruz de la Fuente published in 1907, there were forty letters. In the second edition of 1914, there were fifty-two. The letter is the number also published in the *Obras*, vol. 6. The Gómez de la Serna edition gives only a selection, but this is the only version easy to obtain. A selection was also published in English translation in Mexico City (trans. Dorrey Malcolm) with an introduction by José Antonio Portuondo (Havana: Juan Fernández Burgos, 1956) The *Diario de amor* (Madrid: Aguilar, 1928) contains letters culled from the Cruz de la Fuente edition, despite the spurious claims of the editor Alberto Ghiraldo.

Selected Bibliography

PRIMARY SOURCES

1. Collected and other editions

Antología, poesías y cartas amorosas. Introduction by Ramón Gómez de la Serna. Buenos Aires: Espasa Calpe, 1945.

El aura blanca, leyenda. Notes by Isreal M. Moliner. Matanzas, 1959.

Autobiografía y cartas de la illustre poetisa hasta ahora inéditas. Introduction by D. Lorenzo Cruz de Fuentes. Huelva: Imprenta Miguel Mora, 1907. Reissued in *Cuba Contemporánea,* introduction by Carlos de Velasco (Havana: Imprenta el Siglo XX, 1914); reissued with the title *Autobiografía y cartas (Hasta ahora inéditas),* 2d ed. (Madrid: Imprenta Helénica, 1914).

Cartas inéditas y documentos relativos a su vida en Cuba de 1859 a 1864. Illustrated by José Augusto Escoto. Matanzas: Imprenta La Pluma de Oro, 1912.

Diario de amor. Introduction by Alberto Ghiraldo. Madrid: Aguilar, 1928.

Cartas inéditas de la Avellaneda. Edited by Domingo Figarola-Caneda. In *La Familia.* Havana, 1878–1879.

Gertrudis Gómez de Avellaneda, bibliografía e iconografía. Edited by Domingo Figarola-Caneda. Madrid: Sociedad General, de Librería, 1929.

Obras literarias de la señora doña Gertrudis Gómez de Avellaneda. 5 vols. Madrid: Imprenta de M. Rivadenera, 1868. Vol. 1: Poesía lírica; Vols. 2–3: Obras dramáticas (vol. 2, 1869; *Munio Alfonso, El Príncipe de Viana, Recaredo, Saúl, Baltasar, Catalina;* vol. 3: *La hija de la flores o todos están locos, La aventurera, Oráculos de Talía o los duendos en palacio, La hija del rey René, El millonario y la maleta, La verdad vence apariencias, Tres amores);* Vol. 4: *El artista barquero o los cuatro cinco de junio, Espatolino, Dolores.*

Obras dramáticas de doña Gerturdis Gómez de Avellaneda. 2 vols. Madrid, 1877. These reproduce vols. 2–3 of the above edition.

Obras de doña Gertrudis Gómez de Avellaneda. 6 vols. Centennial edition. Havana: Imprenta de A. Miranda, 1914. Vol. 1: Poesías líricas; Vol. 2–3: as in the first edition; Vol. 4: adds *Sab*; Vol. 5: *Dos mujeres, Guatimocín, el último emperador de México, La velada del helecho o el donativo del diablo, La bella Toda y los doce jabalíes, La montaña maldita, La flor del angel, La ondina del lago azul, La Dama de Amboto, El aura blanco, La Baronesa de Joux, El cacique de Turmequé*; Vol. 6: *Mi última excursión a los pirineos, Páginas críticas, Aspasia, Catalina II, Apuntes biográficos de la Señora Condesa de Merlín, Carta-Prólogo* (a *La anatomía de un corazón*) *Carta-Prólogo* (a *Las lecciones del mundo*), *Carta-Prólogo* (a las *Poesías* de Luisa Pérez de Zambrana), *Carta patriótica, La mujer, Autobiografía y cartas, Tabla de variantes en las poesías líricas,* · *La Avellaneda ante la crítica, Composición dedicada a la Avellanela.*

Obras de Gertrudis Gómez de Avellaneda. Biblioteca de Autores Españoles. D. José María Castro y Calvo. Madrid: Atlas, 1974 (vol. 272), 1978 (vol. 278), 1979 (vol. 279). Vol. 272 contains a lengthy study, letters, bibliography, and the *Poesía lírica*; Vol. 278 the *Obras dramáticas: Munio Alfonso, El príncipe de Viana, Recaredo, Saúl, Baltasar and Catalina*; Vol. 279 also contains Obras dramáticas: *Egilona, El donativo del diablo, La hija de las flores, La aventurera, Oráculos de Talia*. Presumably the B.A.E. series will continue with the novels and short prose, but no publication date is presently available.

Poesías líricas de la Señora Doña Gertrudis Gómez de Avellaneda. Madrid: Leocadio López, 1877. Prologue by Juan Nicasio Gallego for the first edition of the poems.

Poesías selectas. Introduction by D. Benito Varela Jácome. Barcelona: Editorial Breguera, 1956.

Sab: Novela. Havana: Consejo Nacional de Cultura, 1965.

Sab. Introduction by Carmen Bravo Villasante. Salamanca: Anaya, 1970.

Selección poética. Havana: Dirección de Cultura de la Secretaría de Educación, 1936.

Teatro de Gertrudis Gómez de Avellaneda. Introduction by J. A. E. Havana: Consejo Nacional de Cultura: 1965. Contains *Munio Alfonso, Saúl, La hija de las flores, El millonario y la maleta,* and a lengthy bibliography.

Teatro cubano de siglo XIX, Antología. Introduction by Natividad González Freire. Havana: Editorial Arte y Literatura, 1975. Vol. 2: *Munio Alfonso, Baltasar, Tres amores.*

2. Translations

Belshazzar. Translated by William Freeman Burbank. London: B.F. Stevens and Brown, 1914. A play.

Cuauhtemoc, The Last Aztec Emperor. Translated by Mrs. Wilson W. Blake. Mexico: F. P. Hoeck, 1898. An historical novel.

The Love Letters. Translated by Dorrey Malcolm. Introduction by José Antonio Portuondo. Havana: Juan Fernández Burgos, 1956.

SECONDARY SOURCES

ARAMBURU MACHADO, MARIANO. *Personalidad literaria de Doña Gertrudis Gómez de Avellaneda.* Conferencias pronunicadas en el Ateneo Científico, Literario y Artístico de Madrid en el año 1897. Madrid: Imprenta Teresiana, 1898. Lacks information in the biographical part. Gives brief résumés of works.

BALLESTEROS, MERCEDES. *Vida de la Avellaneda.* Madrid: Ediciones Cultura Hispánica, 1949. Sensitive and perceptive biography of Tula.

BERNAL, EMILIA. "Gertrudis Gómez de Avellanedo. Su Vida y su obra." *Cuba contemporánea*; 37 (1925). Calls la Avellaneda unparallelled.

BLANCHET Y BRITTON, EMILIO. "Gertrudis Gómez de Avellaneda como poetisa lírica y dramática." *Revista de la Facultad de Libros y Ciencias*, (March, 1914). Highly praises the poetry and drama of la Avellaneda and compares her to such figures as Virgil, Horace, and Fray Luis de León.

BRAVO VILLASANTE, CARMEN. *Sab.* Salamanca: Anaya, 1970. Excellent short introduction to Tula's work in general and *Sab* in particular.

————*Una vida romántica, La Avellaneda.* Barcelona: Enrique Granados, 1967. An excellent and very readable biography of Tula based on primary sources and giving insights into the works.

CARLOS, ALBERTO J. "La Avellaneda y la mujer." In *Actas del Tercer Congreso Internacional de Hispanistas*, Mexico City, August 26–31, 1968. Mexico City: El Colegio de México, 1970. A short but interesting discussion of *Dos mujeres* in relation to Madame de Staël's *Corinne* and to works of George Sand.

CHACON Y CALVO, JOSÉ MARIA. *Gertrudis Gómez de Avellaneda. Las influencias castellanas: examen negativo.* Havana: Imprenta Siglo XX, 1914. A study of influence on Tula's work.

COTARELO Y MORI, EMILIO. *La Avellaneda y sus obras; ensayo biográfico y crítico.* Madrid: Tipografía de Archivos, 1930. By far the most complete study of la Avellaneda to date. Gives lengthy quotations from letters, newspaper articles, and the like that are very helpful. Critical judgments on the plays, and especially on the prose works, are not to be relied upon.

GALLEGO, JUAN NICASIO. *Prólogo a la edición de las poesías de Gertrudis Gómez de Avellaneda.* Madrid, 1841. Of particular interest as Gallego was one of Tula's greatest admirers and friends.

GIL Y CARRASCO, ENRIQUE. "Adiciones a la biografía de la Avellaneda de Nicomedes Pastor Díaz." *Obras literarias* by Gertrudis Gómez de Avellaneda. Madrid, 1869. Vol. 1. Also of interest as being from a contemporary fellow writer and admirer of Tula.

LAZO, RAIMUNDO. *Gertrudis Gómez de Avellaneda. La mujer y la poetisa lírica.* México: Editorial Porrúa, 1972. An extensive study of Tula's life in relation to her poetry. Also includes a well-chosen anthology that illustrates his critical points.

―――. *Historia de la literatura cubana.* Mexico City: Universidad Nacional Autónoma, 1974. Has a section of several pages on la Avellaneda's work in general.

MARQUINA, RAFAEL. *Gertrudis Gómez de Avellaneda. La Peregrina.* Havana: Editorial Trópico, 1939. A serious and well written study, utilizing quotations from original sources to make his points.

MÉNDEZ BEJARANO, MARIO. *Tassara: Nueva biografía crítica.* Madrid, 1928. Contains letters from la Avellaneda to Tassara concerning their love affair and the daughter Brenhilde.

PINERA, ESTELA A. "The Romantic Theater of Gertrudis Gómez de Avellaneda." Ph.D. dissertation. New York University, 1974. Spanish text. Concentrates on an analysis of three plays, *Munio Alfonso, Baltasar,* and *La hija de las flores o todos están loros.* Has good discussions of themes and problems in Tula's dramas. A fine bibliography on the dramas, including the plays that were separately printed, and critical articles on openings in Madrid.

WILLIAMS, EDWIN BUCHER. "The Life and Dramatic Works of Gertrudis Gómez de Avellaneda." Ph. D dissertation. Philadelphia: The University of Pennsylvania, 1924. This is a study in English, with quotations from plays in Spanish, of Tula's life and her dramas. Williams confines himself primarily to plot summaries—some not very clear or precise—and makes his most valid contribution on the variants and changes made by Tula in the final edition of the plays.

Index